BALONEY

A TALE IN 3 SYMPHONIC ACTS

PASCAL BLANCHET

DRAWN & QUARTERLY

translated by HELGE DASCHER & JOHN KADLECEK

DRAWN & QUARTERLY

Post Office Box 48056
Montreal, Quebec
Canada H2V 4S8
www.drawnandquarterly.com

First edition: December 2008.
Printed in Canada.

Library and Archives Canada Cataloguing in Publication
Blanchet, Pascal, 1980-
    Baloney : a tale in 3 symphonic acts / Pascal Blanchet;
translated by Helge Dascher.
Translation of: Bologne. Originally published in French by Editions la
Pastèque in 2007.
ISBN 978-1-897299-66-1
    I. Dascher, Helge, 1965- II. Title.
NC1449.B47B6413 2008   741.5'971   C2008-906786-X

Drawn & Quarterly acknowledges the financial contribution of the Government
of Canada through the Book Publishing Industry Development Program (BPIDP)
and the Canada Council for the Arts for our publishing activities and for
support of this edition.

Distributed in the USA by:
Farrar, Straus and Giroux
18 West 18th Street
New York, NY 10011
Orders: 888.330.8477

Distributed in Canada by:
Raincoast Books
9050 Shaughnessy Street
Vancouver, BC V6P 6E5
Orders: 800.663.5714

BALONEY

A TALE IN 3 SYMPHONIC ACTS

ACT I

SETTING

A poor,
isolated town on a high,
rocky peak

ORCHESTRATION
SLOW WALTZ IN A MINOR KEY

- Bass for gravity
- Flute for the wind
- Vibraphone for mystery and snow
- Cellos for austerity
- Oboe for melancholy

THERE ONCE
WAS A TOWN
SET ATOP
A ROCKY CLIFF,
WHERE SNOW
DANCED WITH GLOOM
IN A
NEVER-ENDING
BALL.

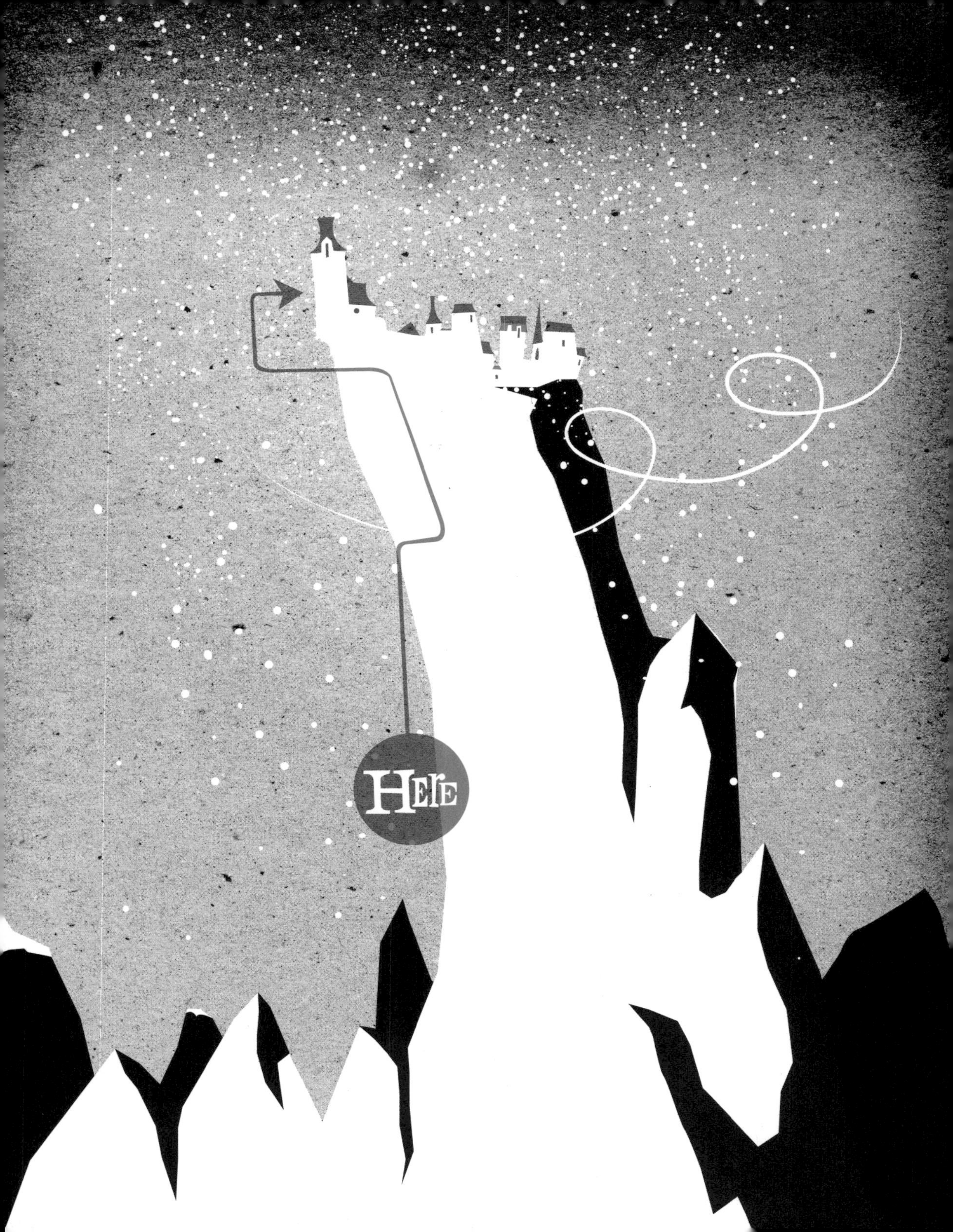
Here

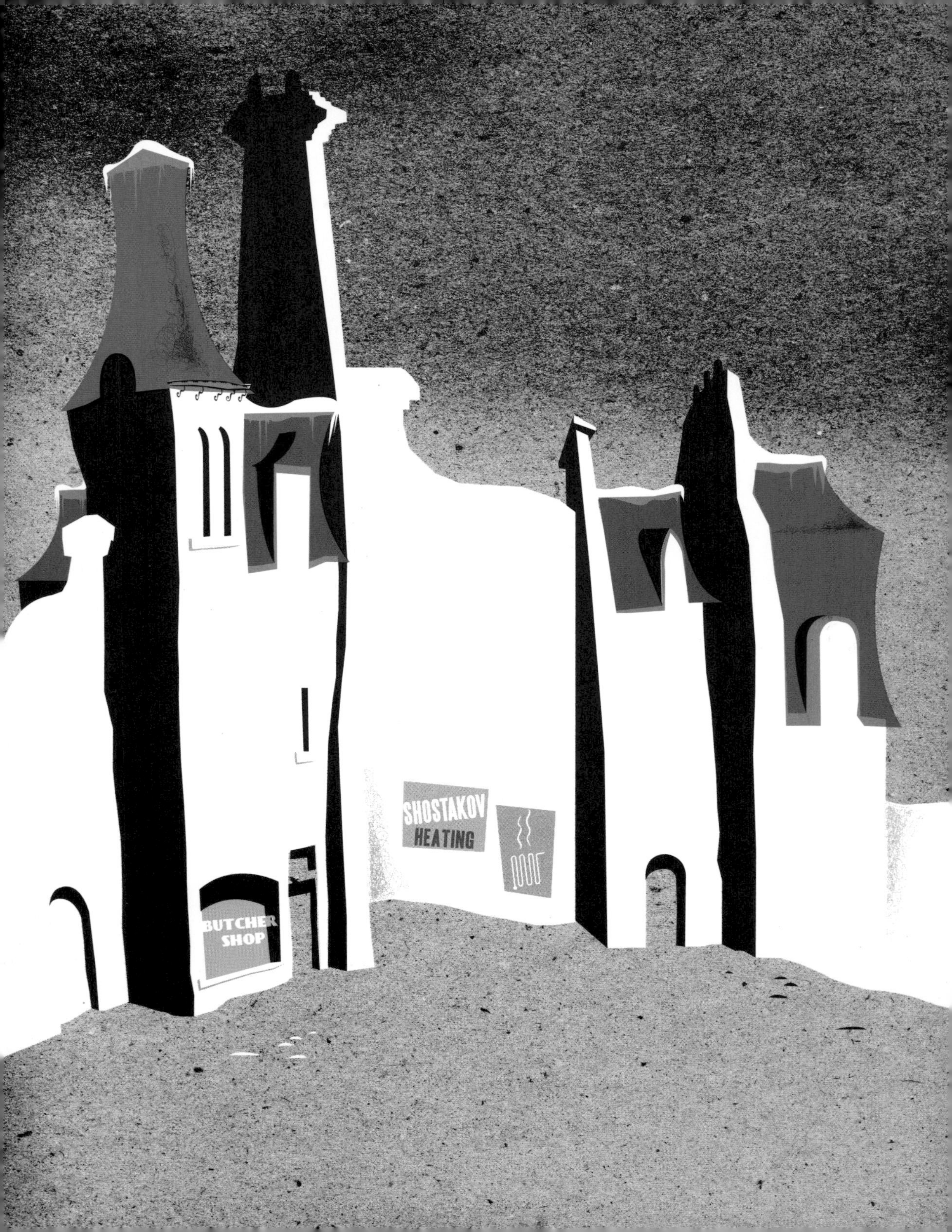
SHOSTAKOV
HEATING
BUTCHER
SHOP

ON THE SOUTHERN EDGE OF TOWN

THERE LIVED A BUTCHER,

A SMALL MAN BURDENED BY THE SORROWS

LIFE HAD DEALT HIM.

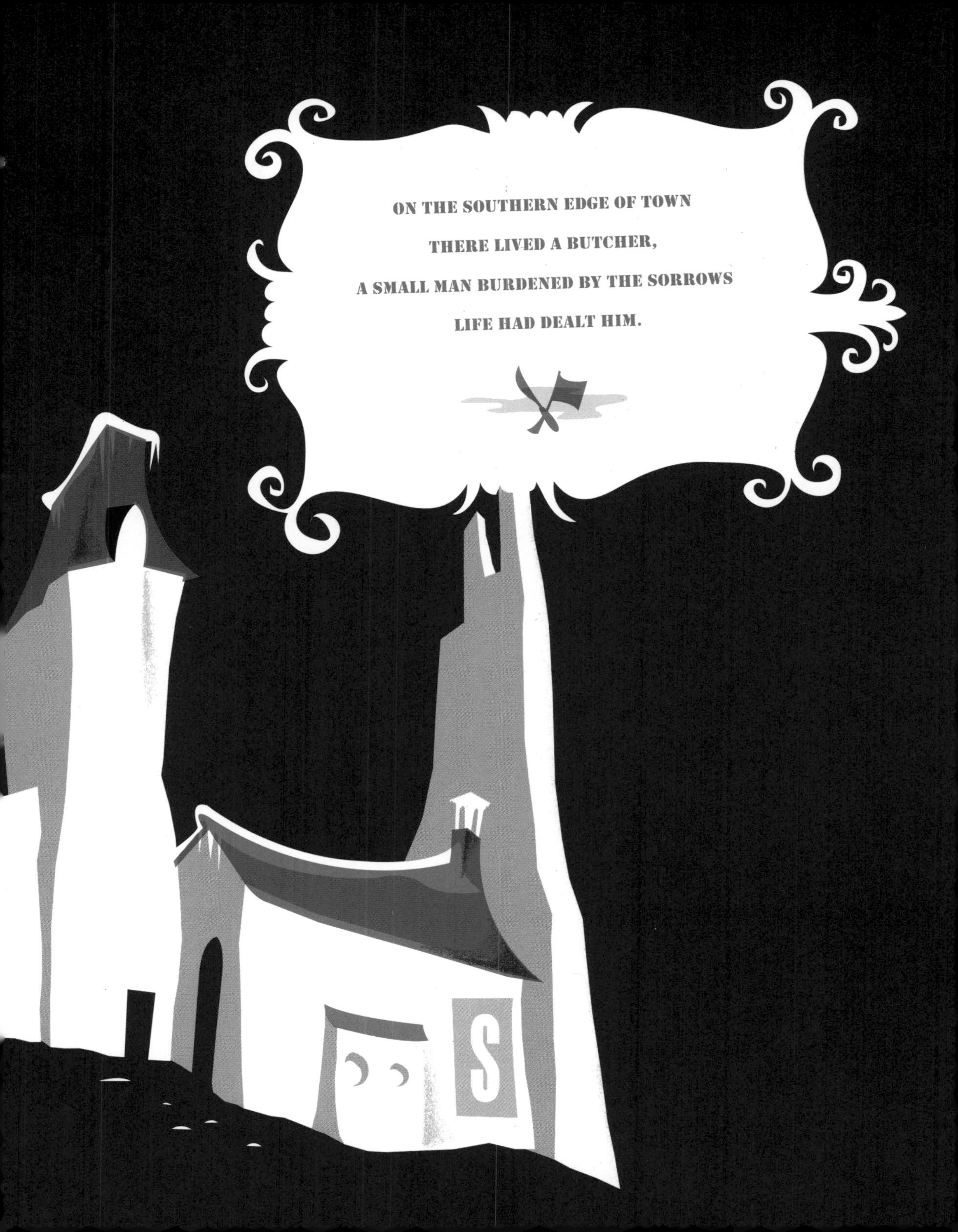
S

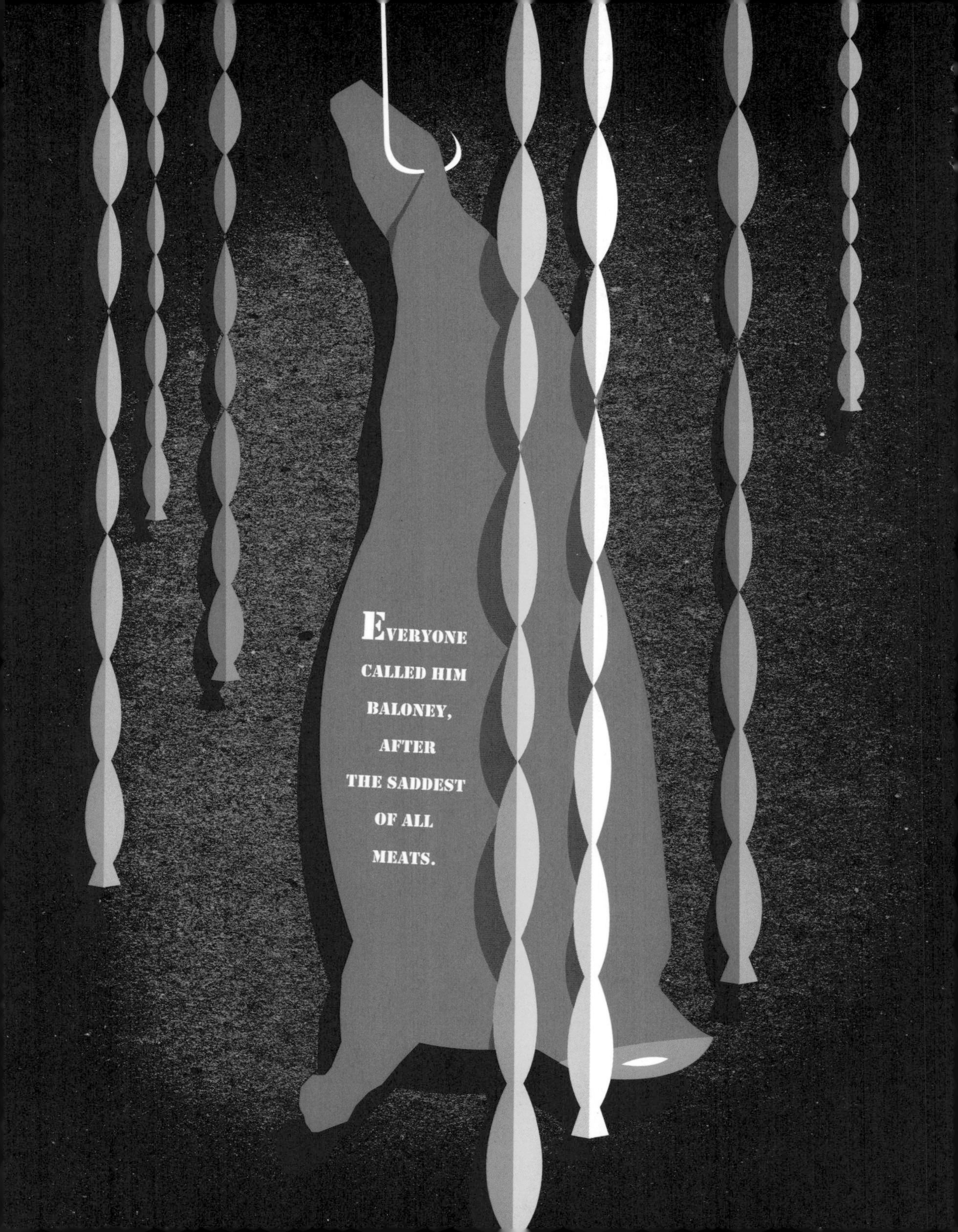

EVERYONE CALLED HIM BALONEY, AFTER THE SADDEST OF ALL MEATS.

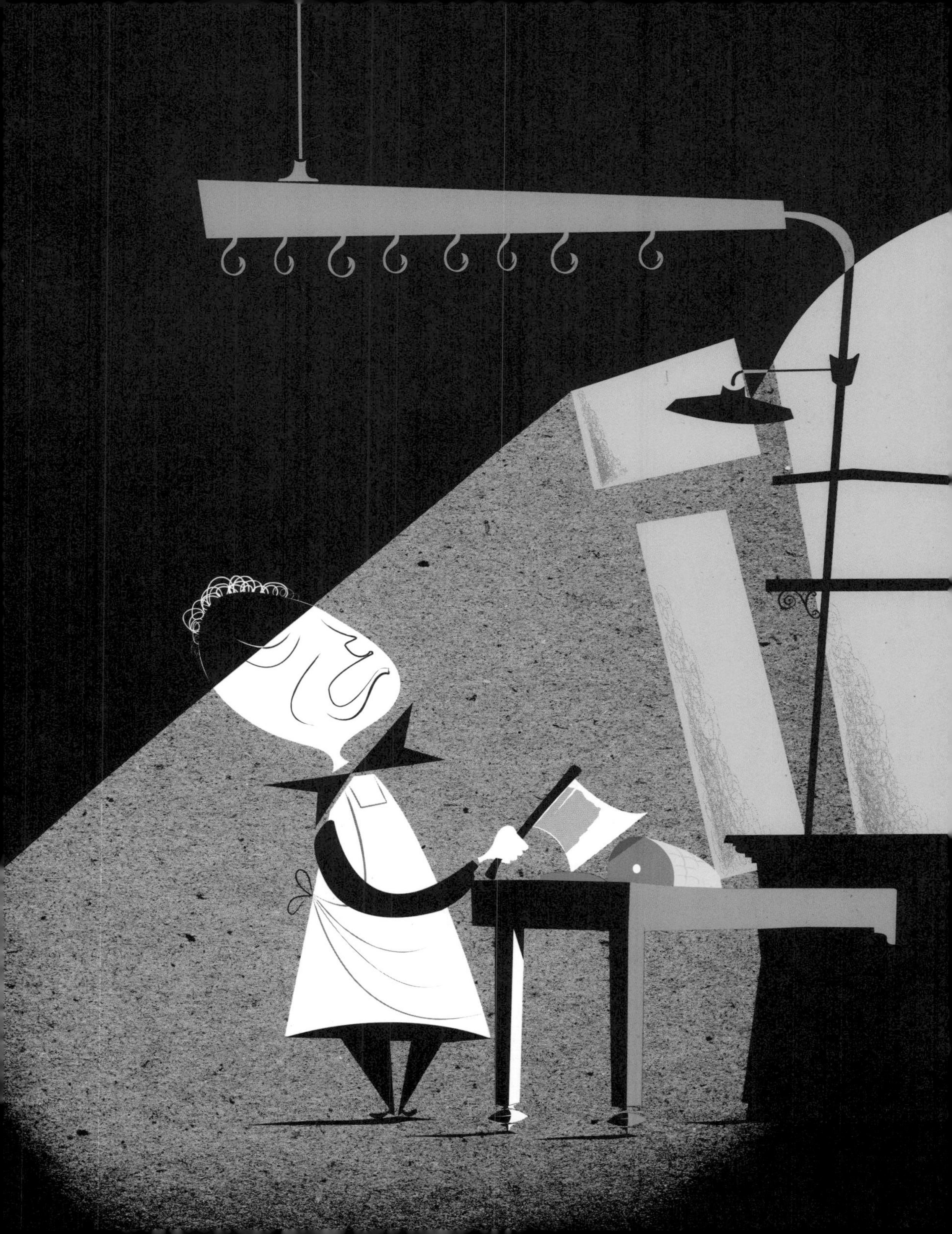

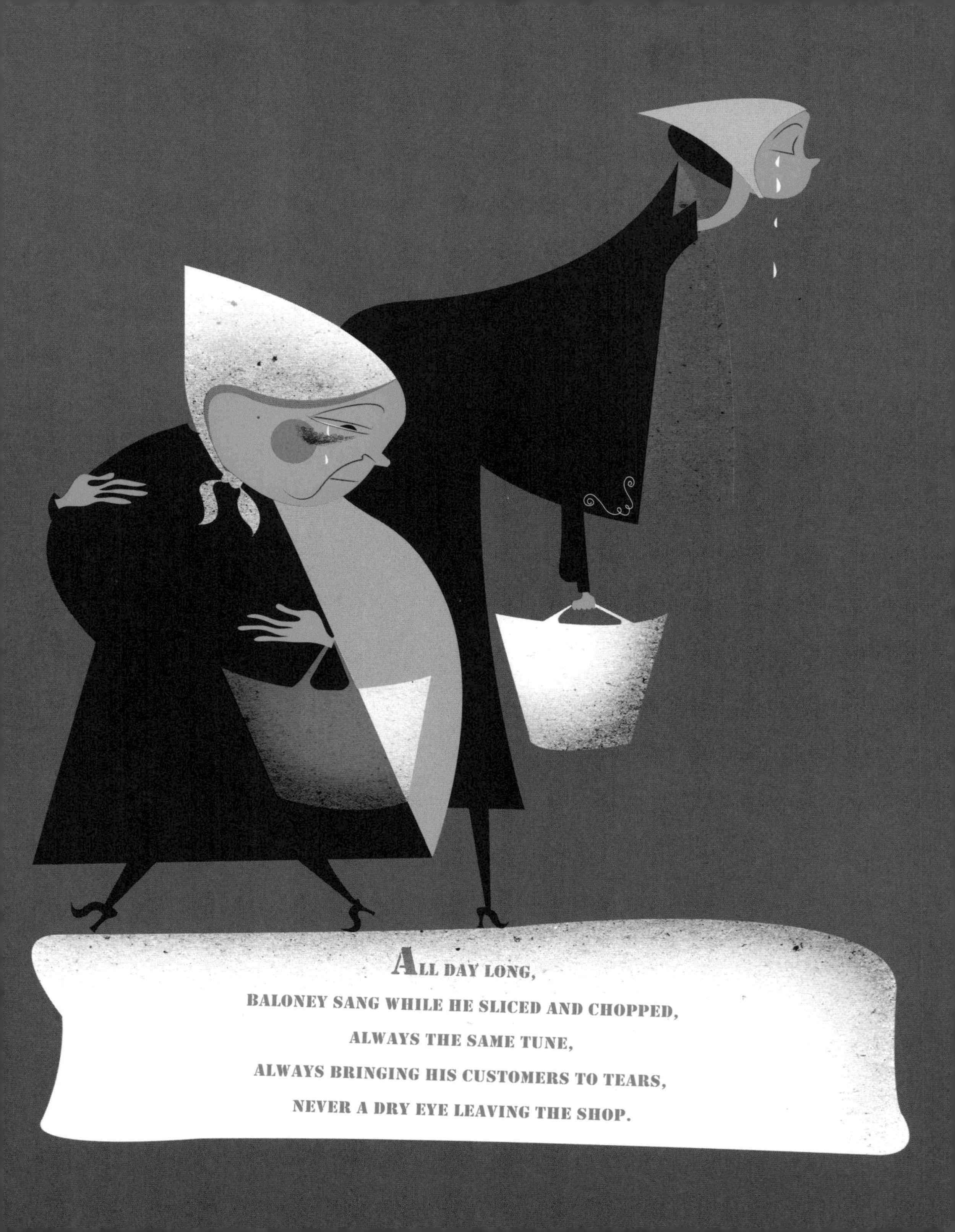

All day long,
Baloney sang while he sliced and chopped,
always the same tune,
always bringing his customers to tears,
never a dry eye leaving the shop.

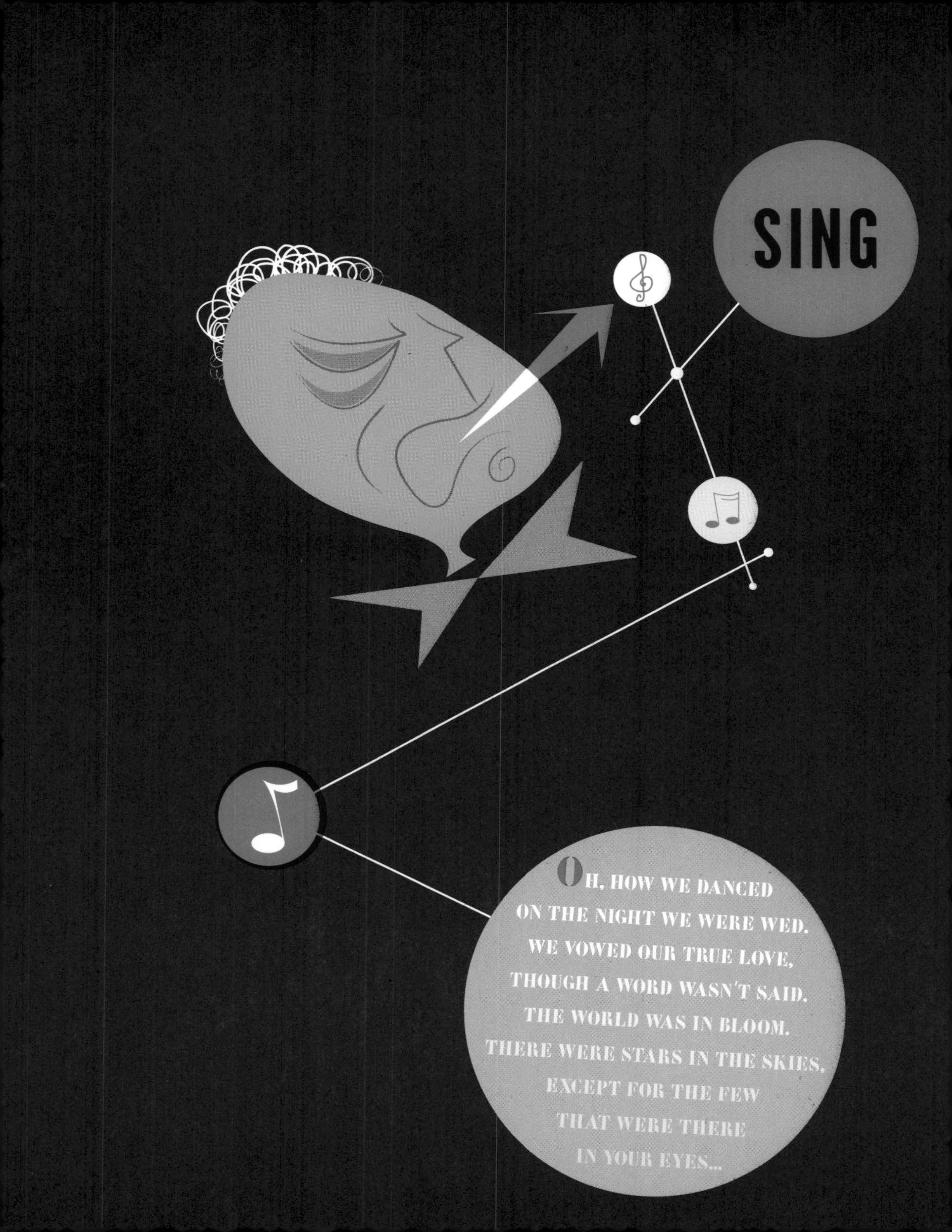
SING

OH, HOW WE DANCED
ON THE NIGHT WE WERE WED.
WE VOWED OUR TRUE LOVE,
THOUGH A WORD WASN'T SAID.
THE WORLD WAS IN BLOOM.
THERE WERE STARS IN THE SKIES,
EXCEPT FOR THE FEW
THAT WERE THERE
IN YOUR EYES...

Baloney had a daughter.
Tragedy played thief to his love and joy
when she was two, stealing her arm in an accident.
A few years later, polio
attacked her leg,
and recently cataracts
had taken her sight.

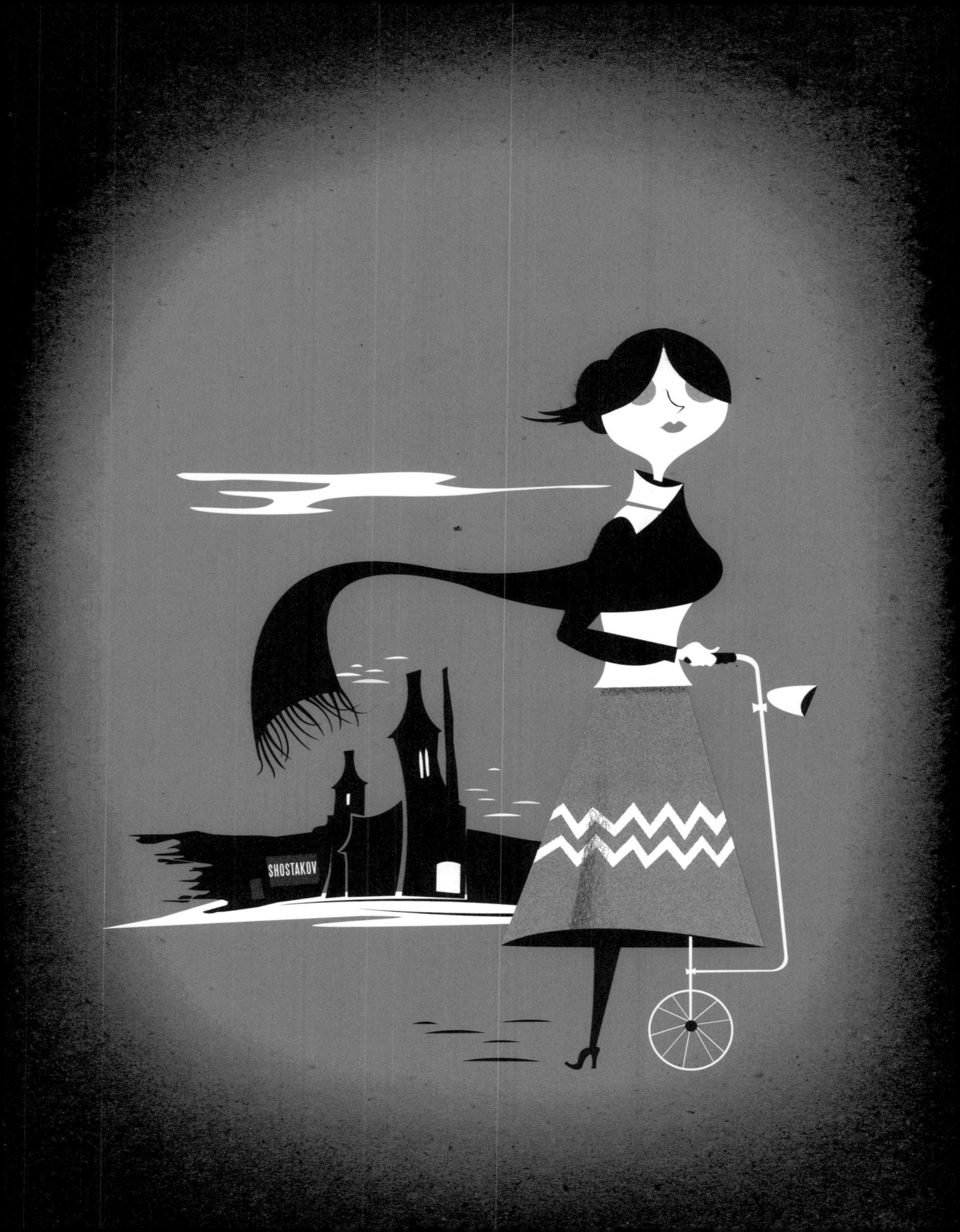
SHOSTAKOV

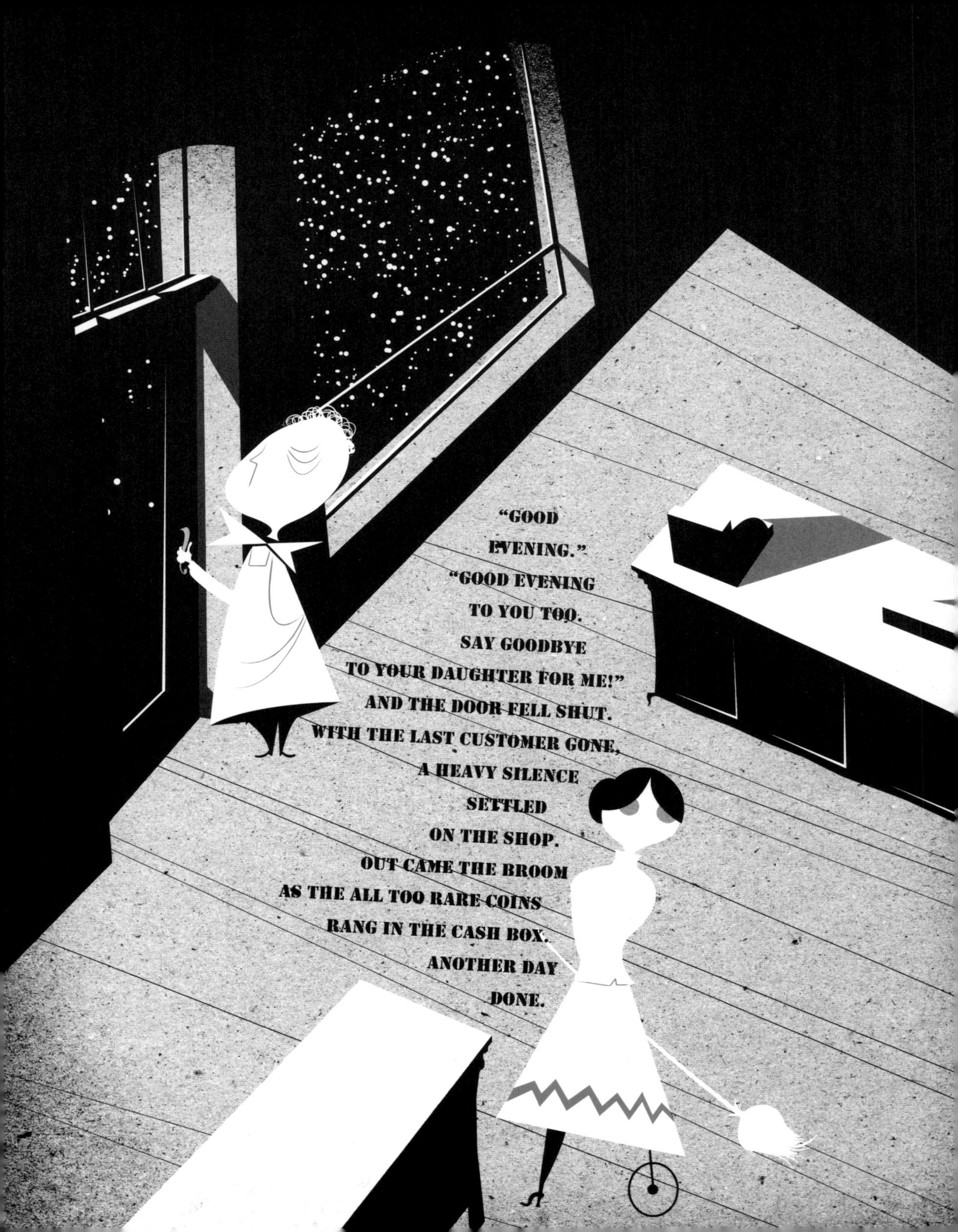

"GOOD
EVENING."
"GOOD EVENING
TO YOU TOO.
SAY GOODBYE
TO YOUR DAUGHTER FOR ME!"
AND THE DOOR FELL SHUT.
WITH THE LAST CUSTOMER GONE,
A HEAVY SILENCE
SETTLED
ON THE SHOP.
OUT CAME THE BROOM
AS THE ALL TOO RARE COINS
RANG IN THE CASH BOX.
ANOTHER DAY
DONE.

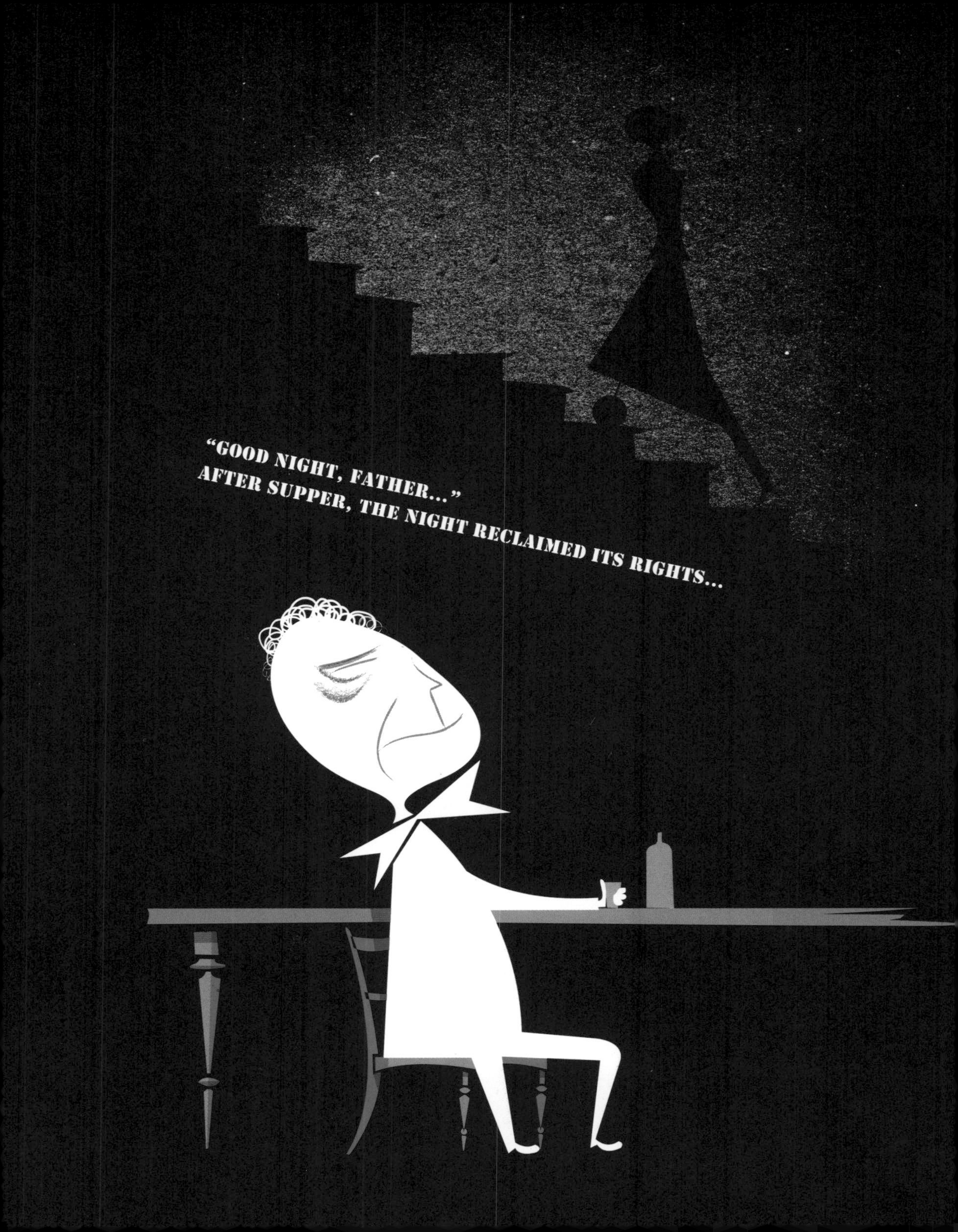
"GOOD NIGHT, FATHER..."
AFTER SUPPER, THE NIGHT RECLAIMED ITS RIGHTS...

FEVER AND HORROR
KEPT BALONEY COMPANY
TIL DAWN.
BEHIND THE OLD CLICKING PENDULUM
NIGHTMARES LURKED.
THE MOMENT HE FELL ASLEEP,
IT ALL CAME BACK...
THAT TRAGIC MORNING,
THE GRASPING HANDS,
THE CRIES OF DISTRESS.

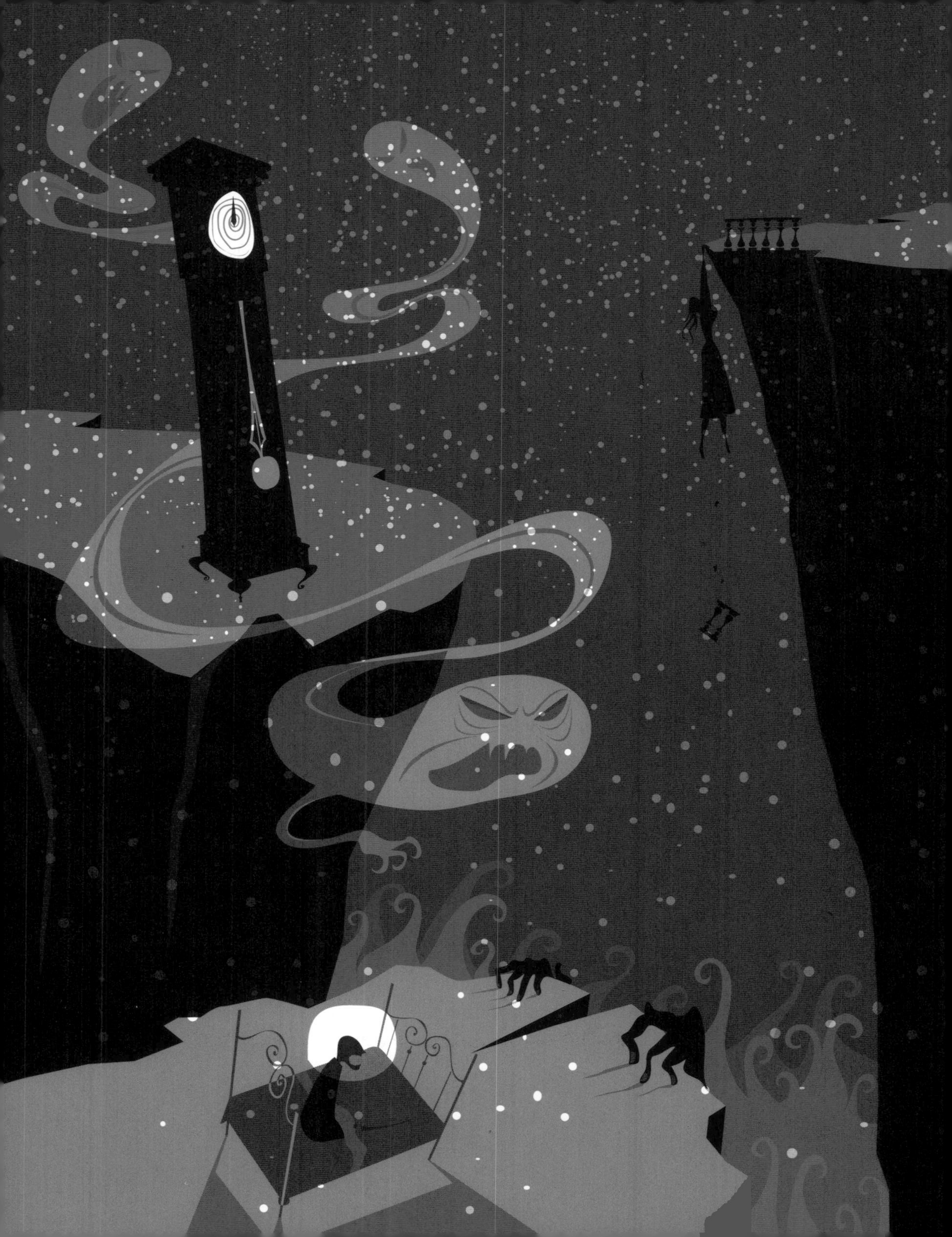

THAT TRAGIC MORNING, THE GRASPING HANDS, THE CRIES OF DISTRESS.

BACK THEN,
BALONEY WAS A HANDSOME YOUNG MAN
AND EVERYONE CALLED HIM BY HIS REAL NAME: SERGEI.
HE HAD GIVEN HIS HEART TO A YOUNG WOMAN,
AND, TWO YEARS EARLIER,
THEY HAD BROUGHT AN ADORABLE BABY GIRL INTO THE WORLD.
THE YOUNG FAMILY BOUGHT THE OLD HOUSE
ON THE SOUTHERN EDGE OF TOWN,
ALONG WITH THE SHOP NEXT DOOR.
BOLONEY PRACTICED HIS TRADE THERE
AND DID A BRISK BUSINESS,
UNTIL THE DAY WHEN TRAGEDY STRUCK.
THAT MORNING THE FAMILY WAS ALL IN THE SHOP—
HIS WIFE, ELBOWS ON THE RAILING OF THE BALCONY IN BACK,
GAZING AT THE EXPANSIVE VIEW OUT OVER THE CLIFF,
HIS DAUGHTER TAGGING ALONG WITH BALONEY
AS HE SLICED AND CHOPPED HIS CUTS OF MEAT.

SUDDENLY,

HE HEARD A DULL THUMP AND CRIES!
HORRIFIED,
BALONEY FLEW TO THE BALCONY,
GRASPED THE HAND OF HIS WIFE
AS SHE DANGLED OVER THE ABYSS,
AND TRIED DESPERATELY TO PULL HER UP WHEN,
GLANCING BACK,
HE GLIMPSED HIS DAUGHTER REACHING TO GRASP
THE RAZOR SHARP CLEAVER HE HAD LEFT
ON THE TABLE.
EVERYTHING HAPPENED IN A BLINK.
BALONEY FLEW BACK TO HIS DAUGHTER
WITHOUT REALIZING HE HAD LET GO OF
THE HAND OF THE WOMAN HE LOVED,
THE WOMAN NOW DISAPPEARING FOREVER INTO THE VOID.
IN THE WAKE OF THIS TRAGEDY,
DUKE SHASTAKOV, THE LOCAL DISPENSER OF JUSTICE,
PRONOUNCED THE SITUATION GRAVE
AND ORDERED THAT A WALL BE BUILT ALL AROUND THE TOWN
AND THAT ALL OPENINGS FACING THE CLIFF BE SEALED.
AS FOR BALONEY,
HE MOVED BEHIND A WALL OF SORROW,
AND LOCKED EVERY DOOR SHUT.

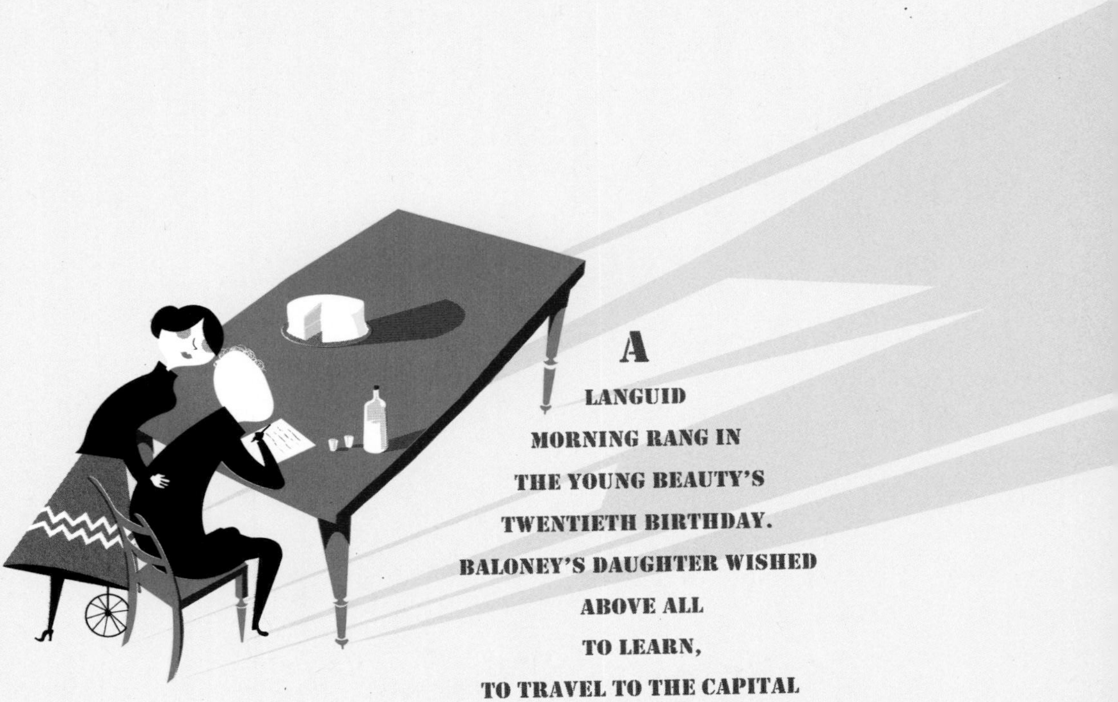

A
LANGUID
MORNING RANG IN
THE YOUNG BEAUTY'S
TWENTIETH BIRTHDAY.
BALONEY'S DAUGHTER WISHED
ABOVE ALL
TO LEARN,
TO TRAVEL TO THE CAPITAL
AND ENTER
ITS TEMPLES OF KNOWLEDGE.
BUT BALONEY KNEW ALL TOO WELL
THAT WITH HER MANY HANDICAPS,
SHE WOULD NEVER
MAKE IT THERE.
READING THE DISAPPOINTMENT
IN HIS DAUGHTER'S EYES,
HE DECIDED TO WRITE A LETTER
TO THE MOST PRESTIGIOUS SCHOOL
IN THE CAPITAL.
HE WOULD REQUEST
A TUTOR BE SENT FROM THE CITY!
HIS APPEAL LEFT IN THE HANDS
OF A COURIER THAT VERY DAY.
WHAT REMAINED OF THE CELEBRATION
WERE THE GIRL'S FAINT HOPE
AND THE WAIT FOR A REPLY.

ACT II

SETTING

The Duke's palace
and the town square

ORCHESTRATION
MINOR KEY WITH A FINALE IN MAJOR

- Brass for arrogance and cruelty
- Bass drum for violence
- Violins for vertigo
- Clarinet for calm

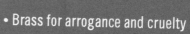

IN THE TOWN,
IT WAS SAID THAT HIS FORTUNE
WAS MATCHED ONLY BY HIS CRUELTY.
THE DUKE PERFORMED
A VARIETY OF FUNCTIONS –
THAT OF JUDGE AND JURY,
INDUSTRIALIST,
ARM OF THE LAW AND,
OF COURSE, DUKE.
ELEGANTLY CLAD,
WITH AN ASSASSIN'S EYE
AND COLD HANDS,
HE RODE THROUGH
THE SMALL TOWN
IN HIS HUGE CARRIAGE,
ALWAYS CAREFUL TO CRUSH
A FEW CHILDREN, TIP OVER
THE RARE SHOP STALL SET OUT IN THE STREET
AND HAND OUT PUNISHMENT
AS HE PLEASED.

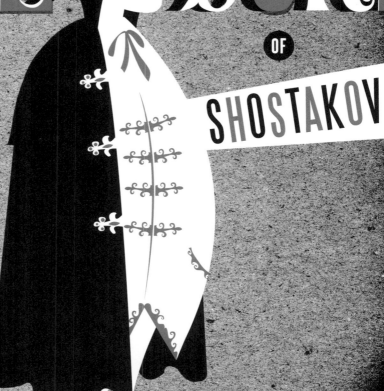

THE DUKE

OF

SHOSTAKOV

IN
HIS PALACE,
THE DUKE WAS ALL
GRANDILOQUENCE.
HERE,
OUT OF SIGHT
OF HIS PEOPLE,
THE DUKE DEPLOYED
THE FULL BOUNTY
OF HIS CHARM.
DID NOT THE COUNTESS
OF KOSTROVKI
SAY OF HIM:
"HE IS
QUITE SIMPLY
A DELICIOUS CREATURE,
A MAN
OF HONOR"?

ME
MY self
and I

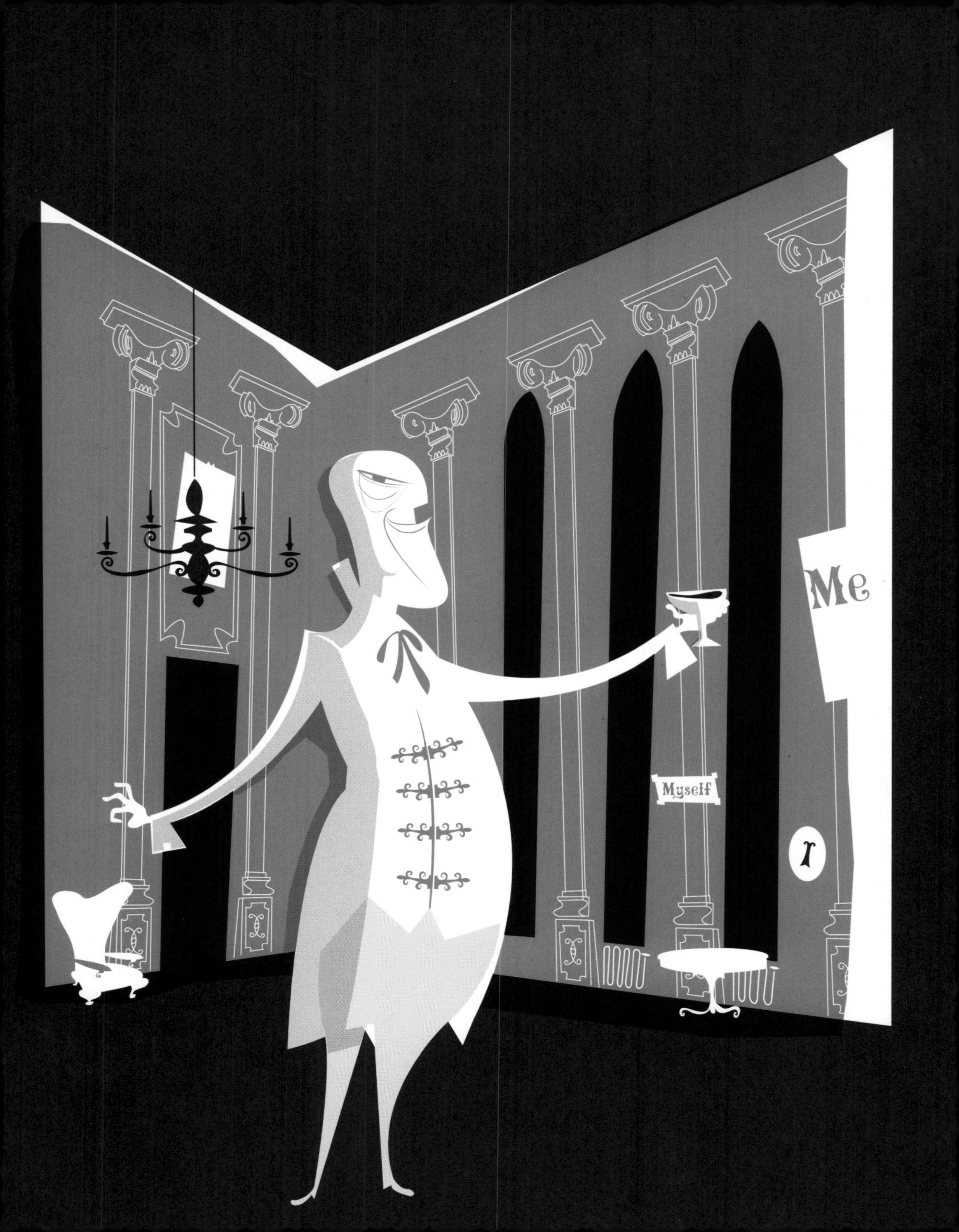
Me
Myself
I

HEAT

SHOSTAKOV

THE DUKE
OWNED
THE ONLY
HEATING
COMPANY
IN TOWN,
MAKING THE MOST
OF THE UNRELENTING
COLD
TO ADD TO HIS
CONSIDERABLE FORTUNE.
THE COST
OF HEATING
ROSE
WITH
PREDICTABLE REGULARITY AND,
IT WAS SAID,
FOR NO GOOD REASON
AT ALL.

COMFORT • SAFETY • COURTESY

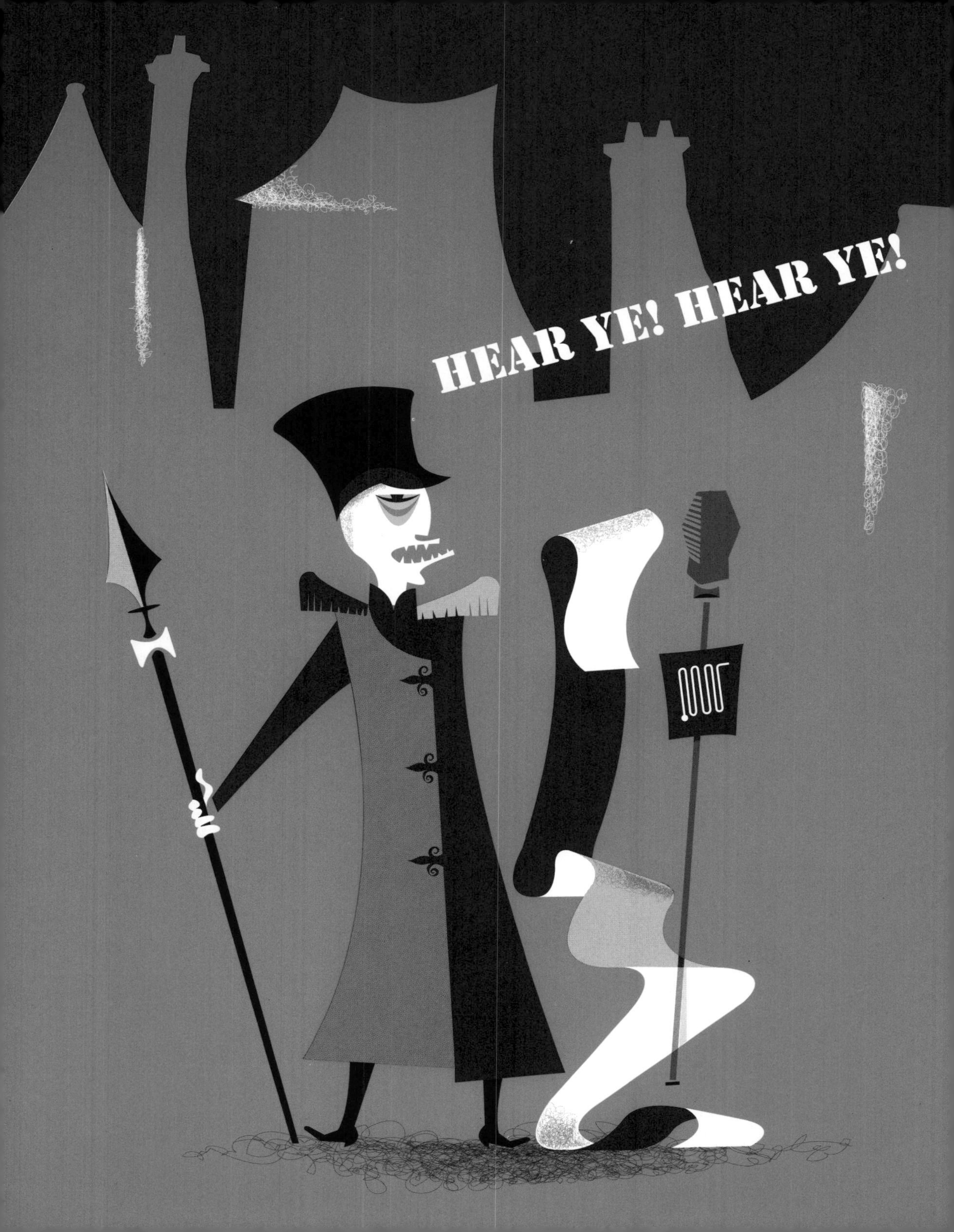
HEAR YE! HEAR YE!

THE YEARS WENT BY IN THE TOWN,
PUNCTUATED BY EXECUTIONS,
SPIKES IN THE COST OF HEATING AND MISERY.
BALONEY'S DAUGHTER HAD SEEN
25 WINTERS COME AND GO...

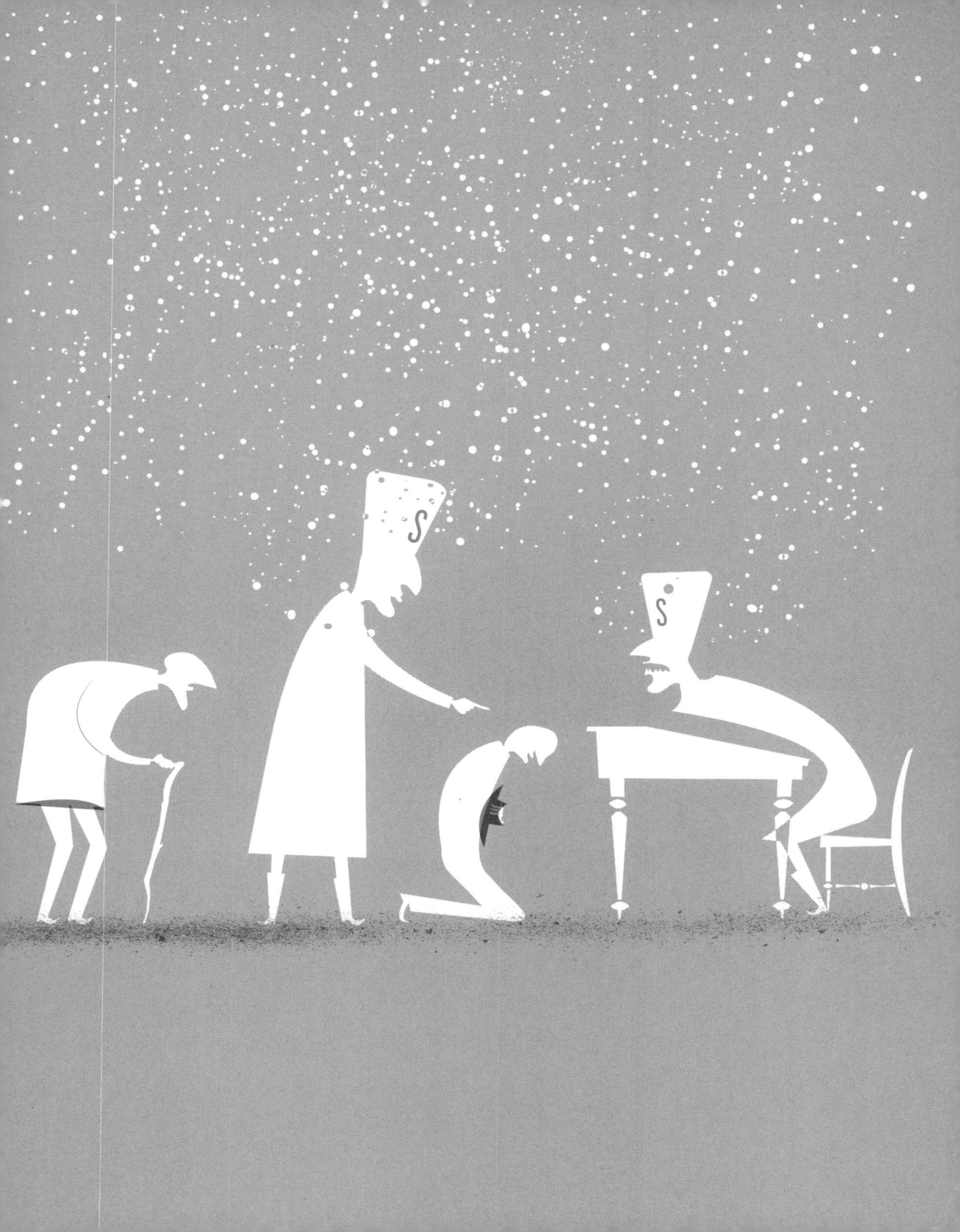
S
S

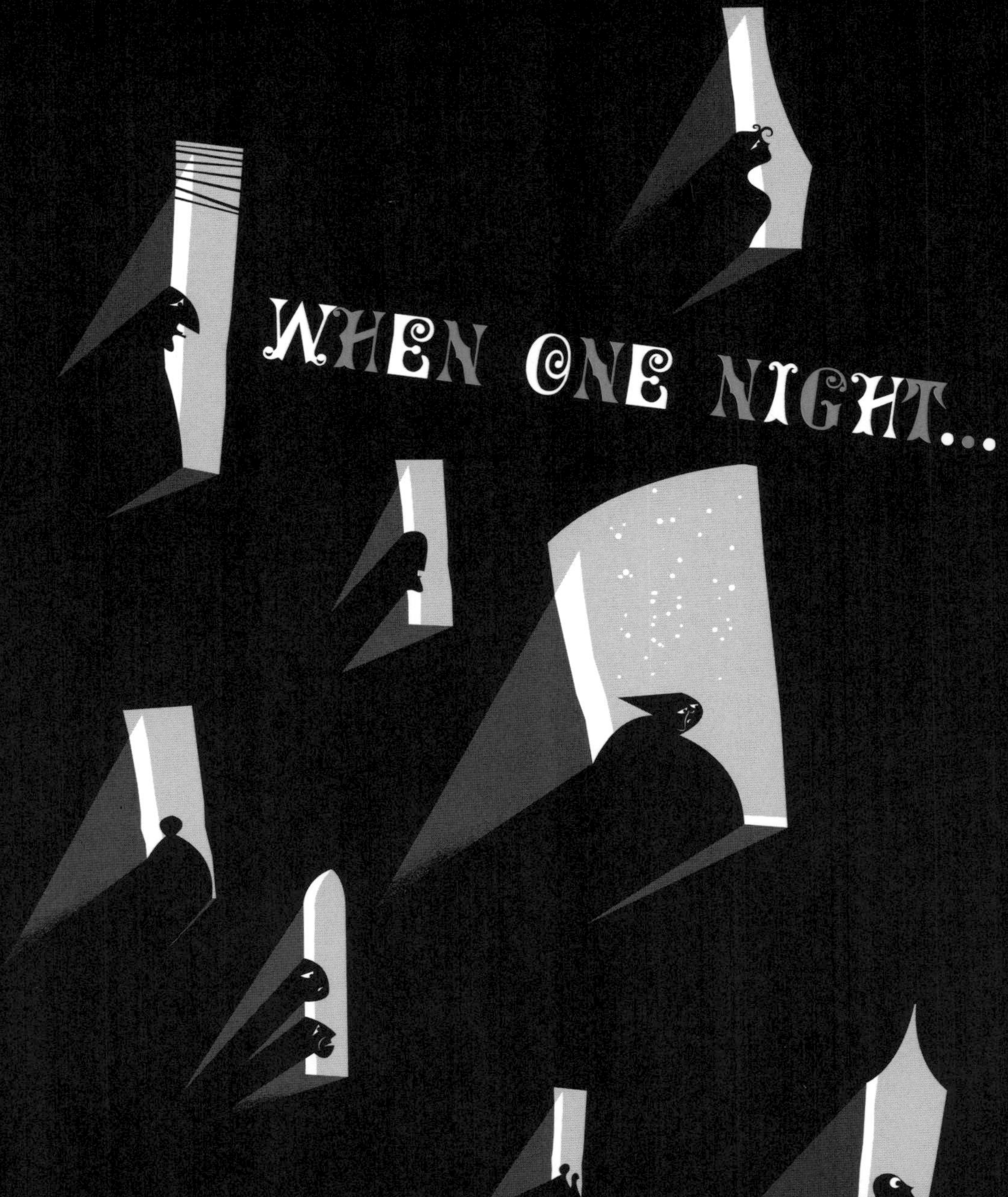
WHEN ONE NIGHT...

THE CLATTER OF HOOFS
COULD BE HEARD IN THE STORM.
A CARRIAGE PULLED UP INTO THE TOWN SQUARE,
THE DOOR OPENED SLOWLY AND
A MAN DRESSED IN BLACK
STEPPED OUT...

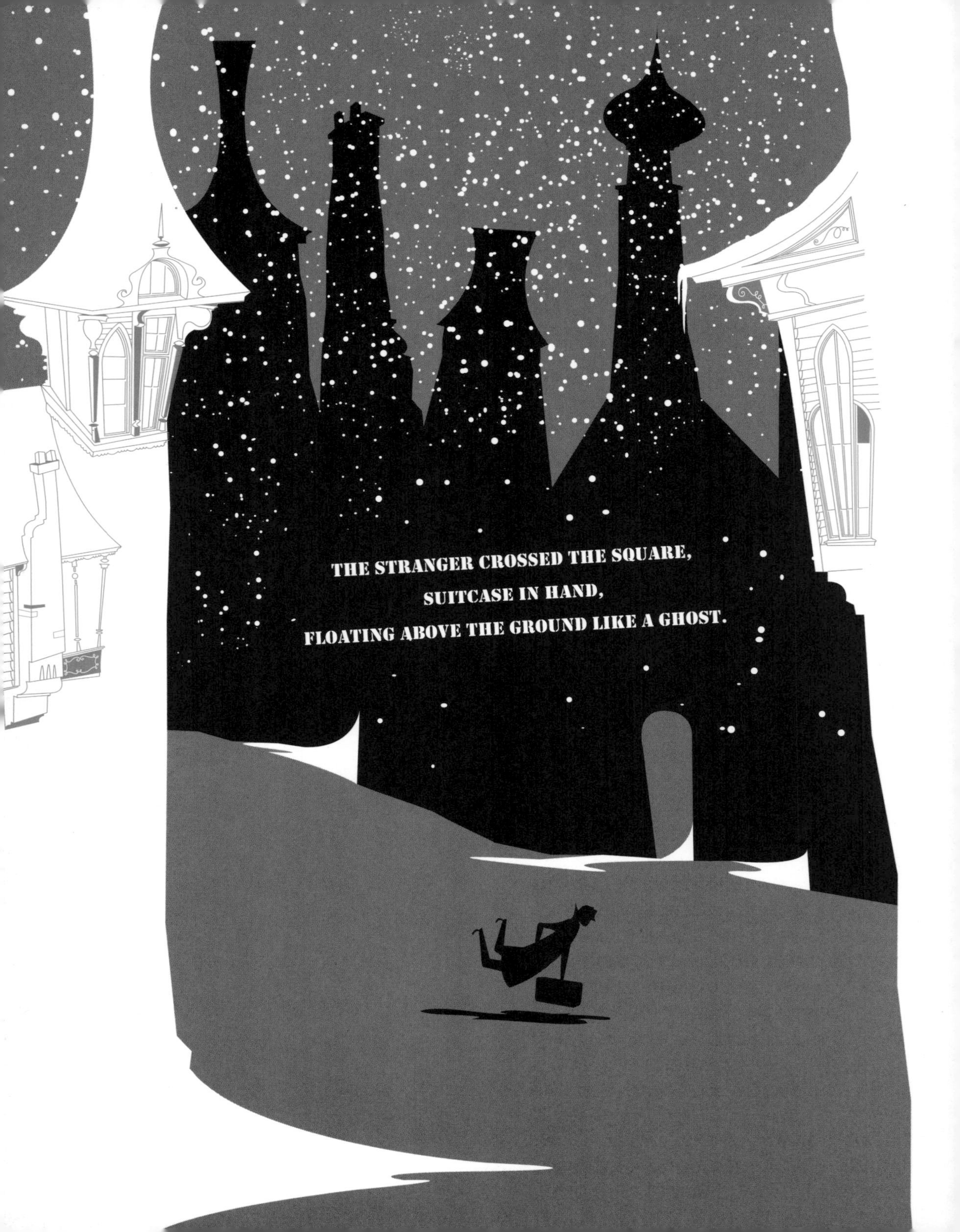
THE STRANGER CROSSED THE SQUARE,
SUITCASE IN HAND,
FLOATING ABOVE THE GROUND LIKE A GHOST.

CASTING A LONG SHADOW OVER ITS HEAVY DOOR,

AND TOOK HOLD OF THE KNOCKER.

THE ECHO OF THREE LOUD KNOCKS

FADED AWAY INTO THE WIND...

BALONEY
WOKE WITH A START
AND HURRIED DOWN THE STAIRS.

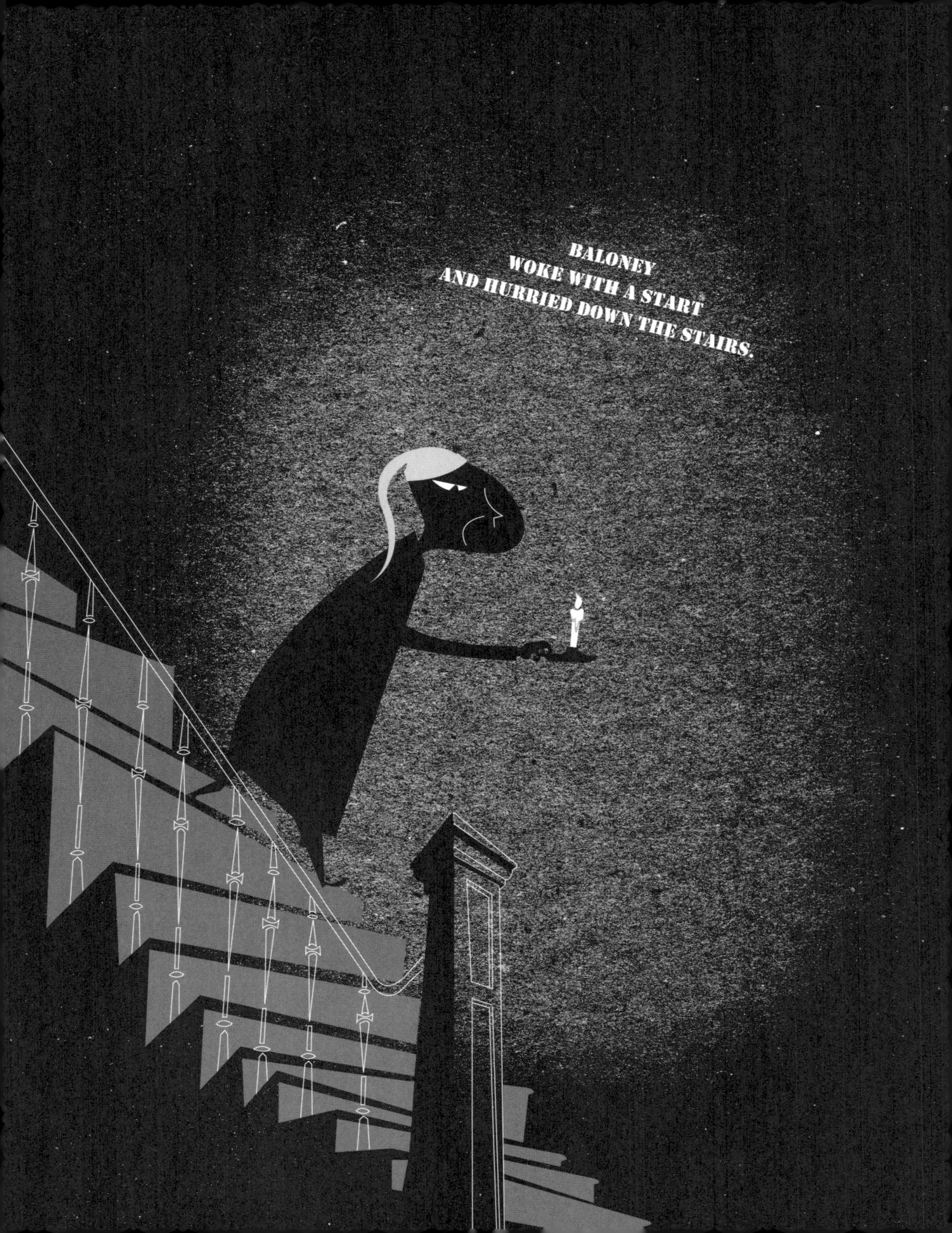

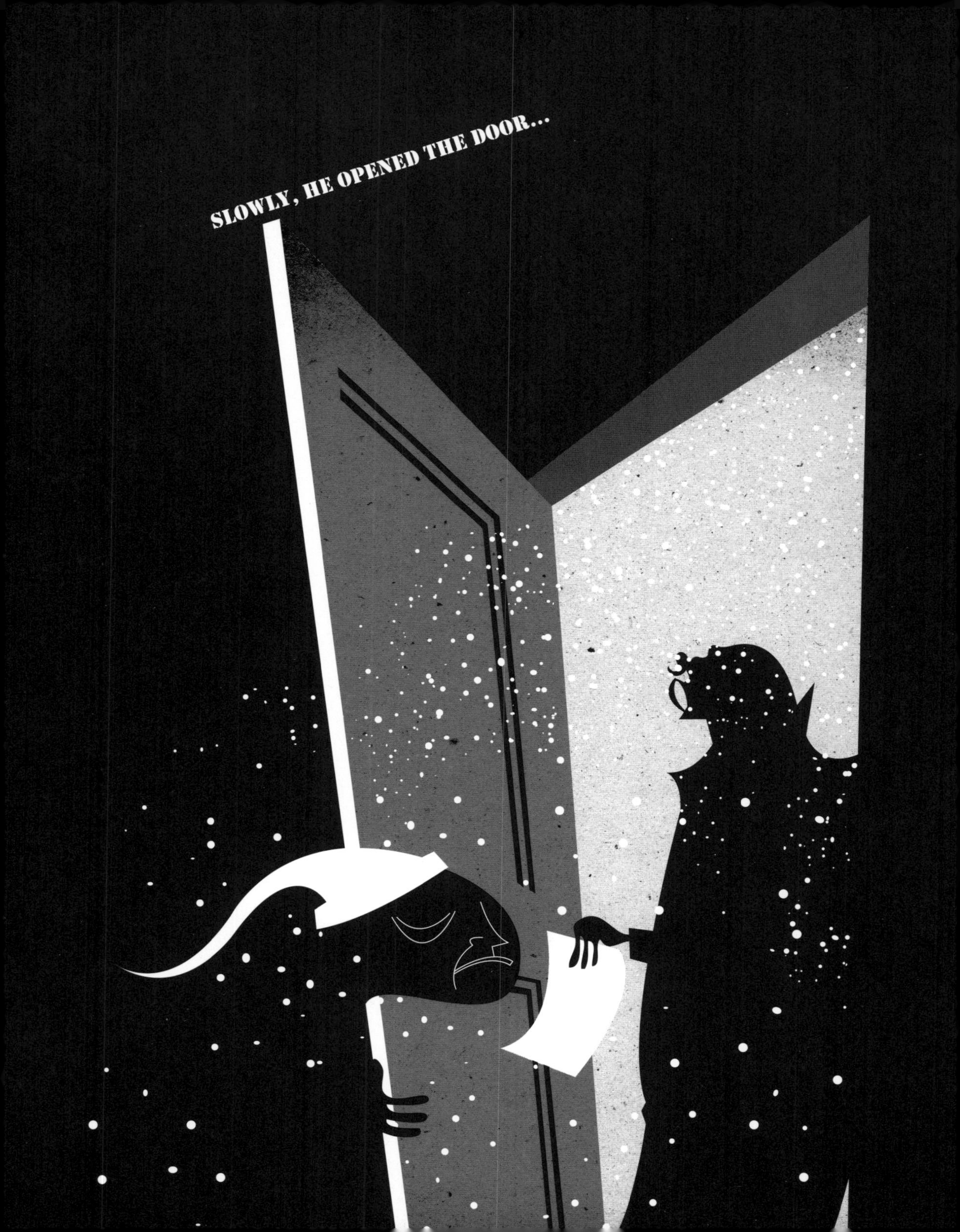
SLOWLY, HE OPENED THE DOOR...

IN THE KITCHEN,
THE DREARINESS OF THE HOUSE
MELTED AWAY
AT THE JOY FELT
BY BALONEY AND HIS DAUGHTER.
THE TUTOR
HAD FINALLY COME!
AFTER FIVE YEARS OF WAITING,
HE WAS HERE,
UNDER THEIR ROOF,
SEATED AT THEIR TABLE.
DRINKING GLASS AFTER GLASS,
THEY LEARNED
WHAT HAD TAKEN SO LONG:
AFTER LONG YEARS OF PASSING
FROM OFFICES TO BOARD ROOMS,
FROM ONE FLOOR AND DEPARTMENT TO THE NEXT,
BALONEY'S LETTER HAD AT LAST
MADE ITS WAY TO THE MAILBOX
OF THE YOUNG TUTOR.
A FEW GLASSES MORE AND
THEY UNDERSTOOD WHY
THE TUTOR'S FEET
DIDN'T TOUCH THE GROUND:
THE MAN WAS
A DREAMER...

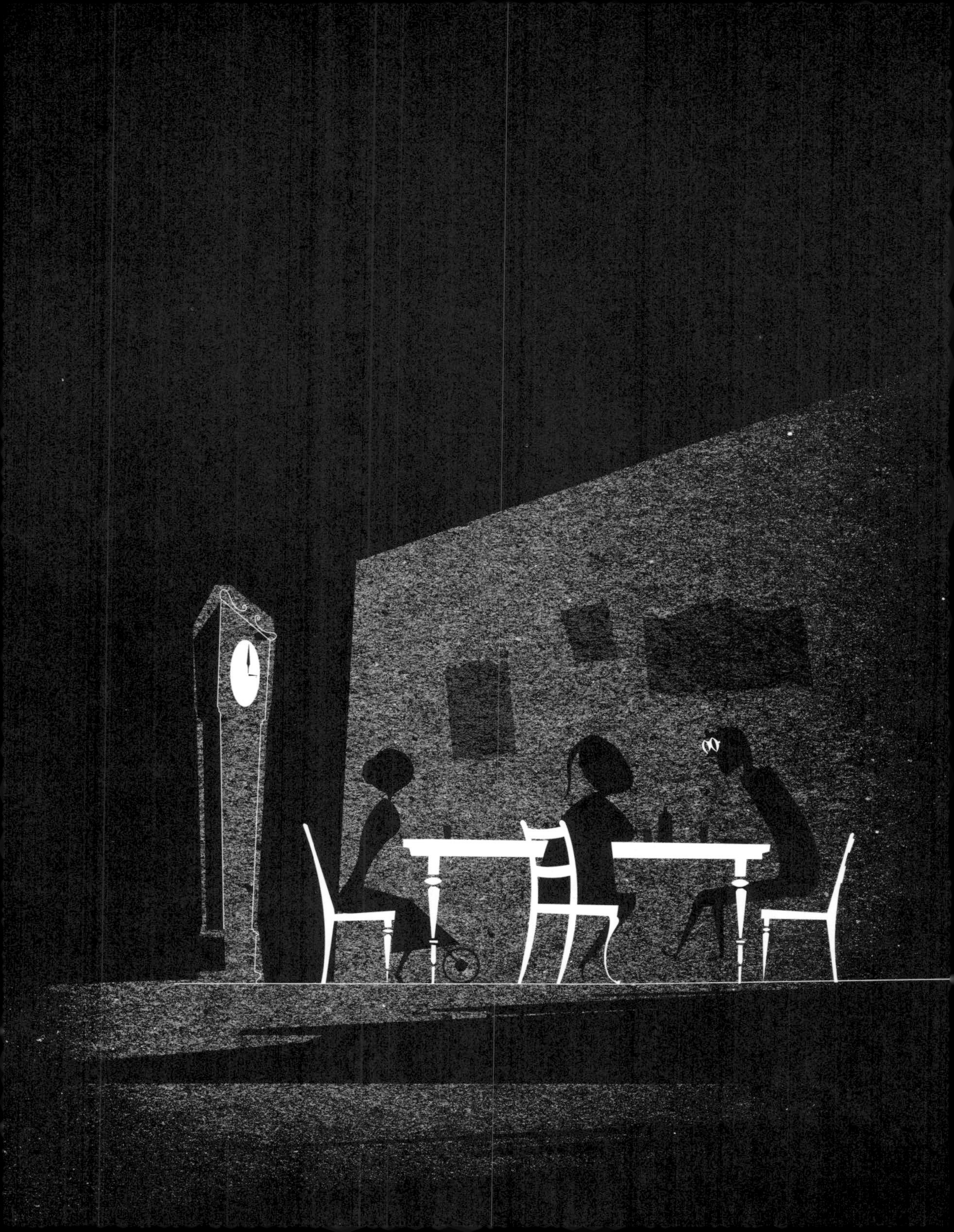

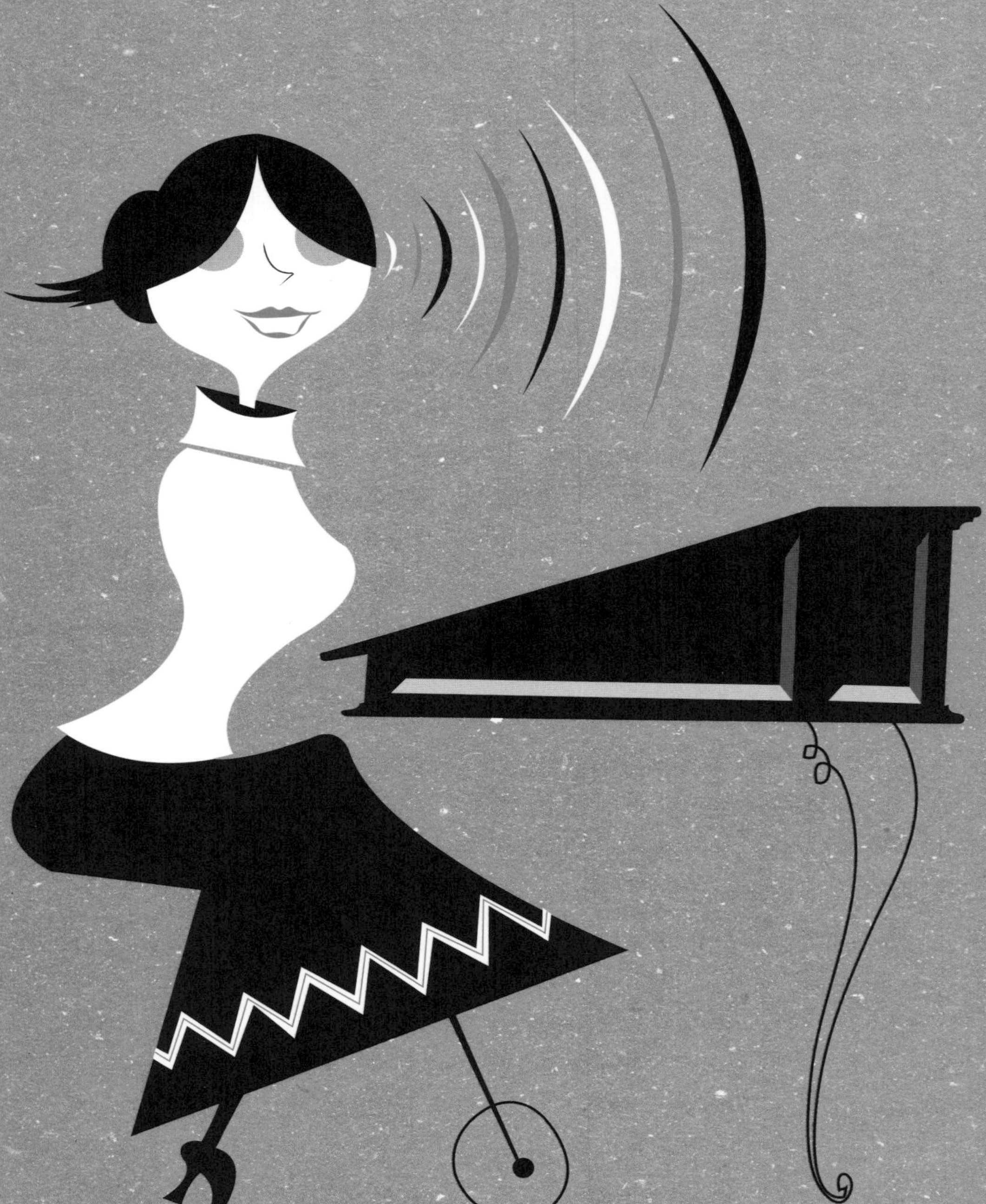

PERFECT PITCH

CLASSES BEGAN
THE NEXT DAY.
THANKS TO THE TUTOR,
THE MOOD IN
THE HOUSE LIGHTENED,
SO THAT
SOME DAYS,
YOU COULD FEEL
JOY LIVING
IN ITS WALLS.

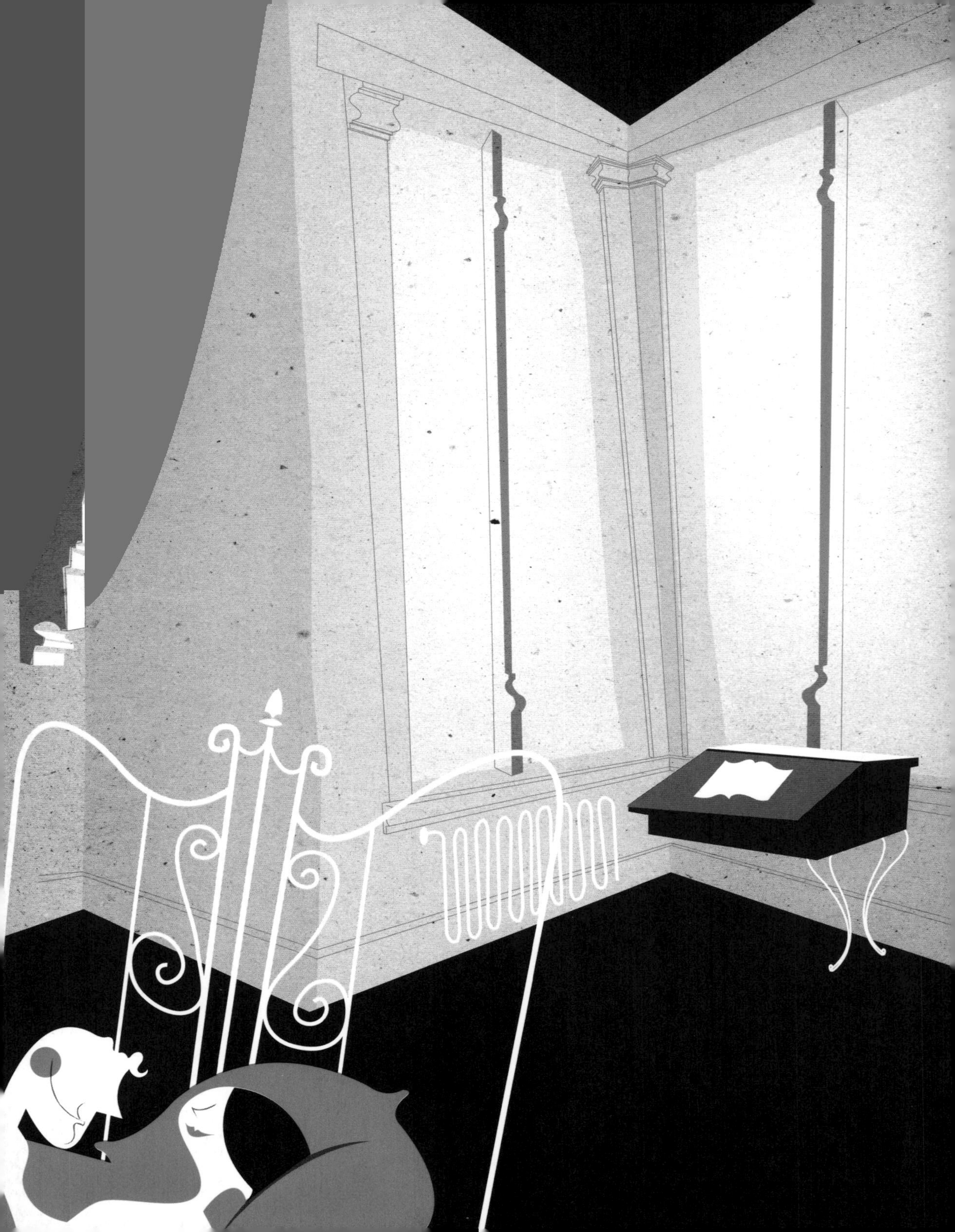

It wasn't long
before learning gave way to passion.
They fell in love...

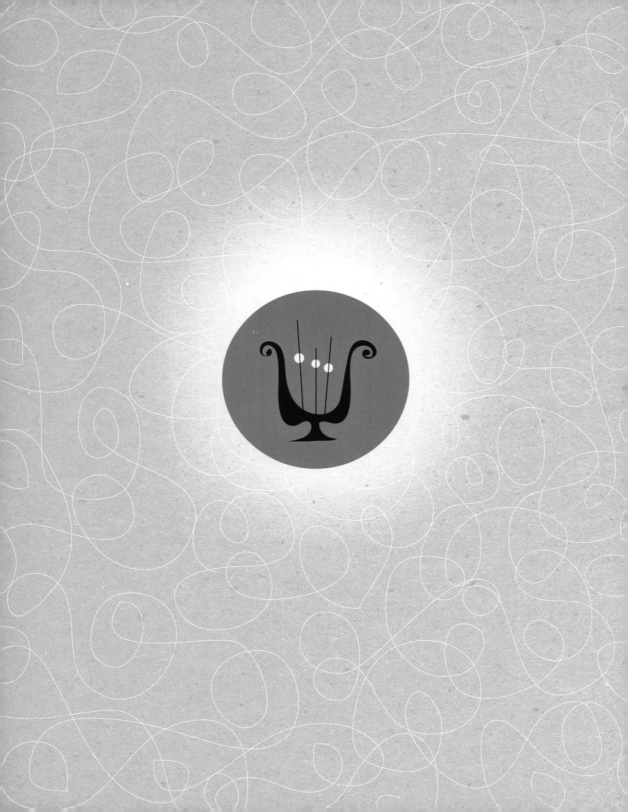

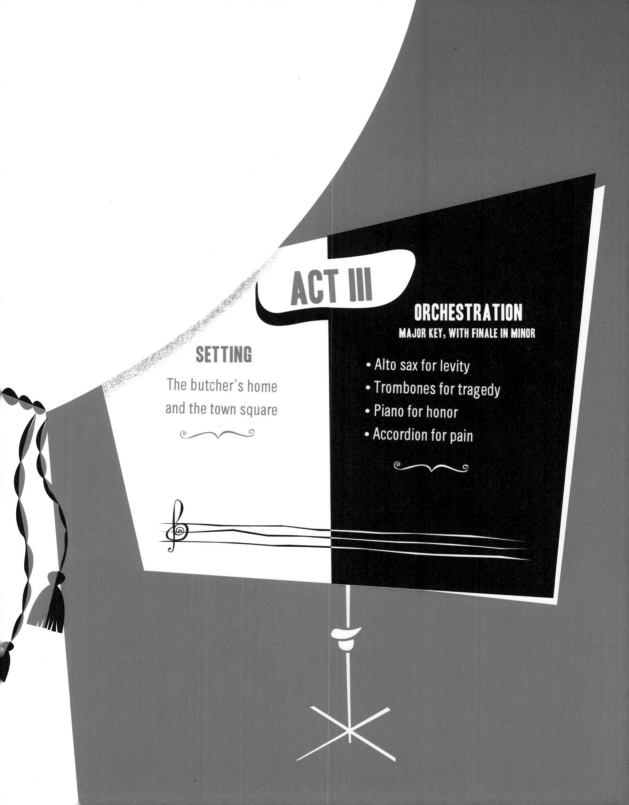

ACT III

SETTING

The butcher's home
and the town square

ORCHESTRATION
MAJOR KEY, WITH FINALE IN MINOR

- Alto sax for levity
- Trombones for tragedy
- Piano for honor
- Accordion for pain

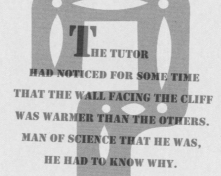

THE TUTOR
HAD NOTICED FOR SOME TIME
THAT THE WALL FACING THE CLIFF
WAS WARMER THAN THE OTHERS.
MAN OF SCIENCE THAT HE WAS,
HE HAD TO KNOW WHY.

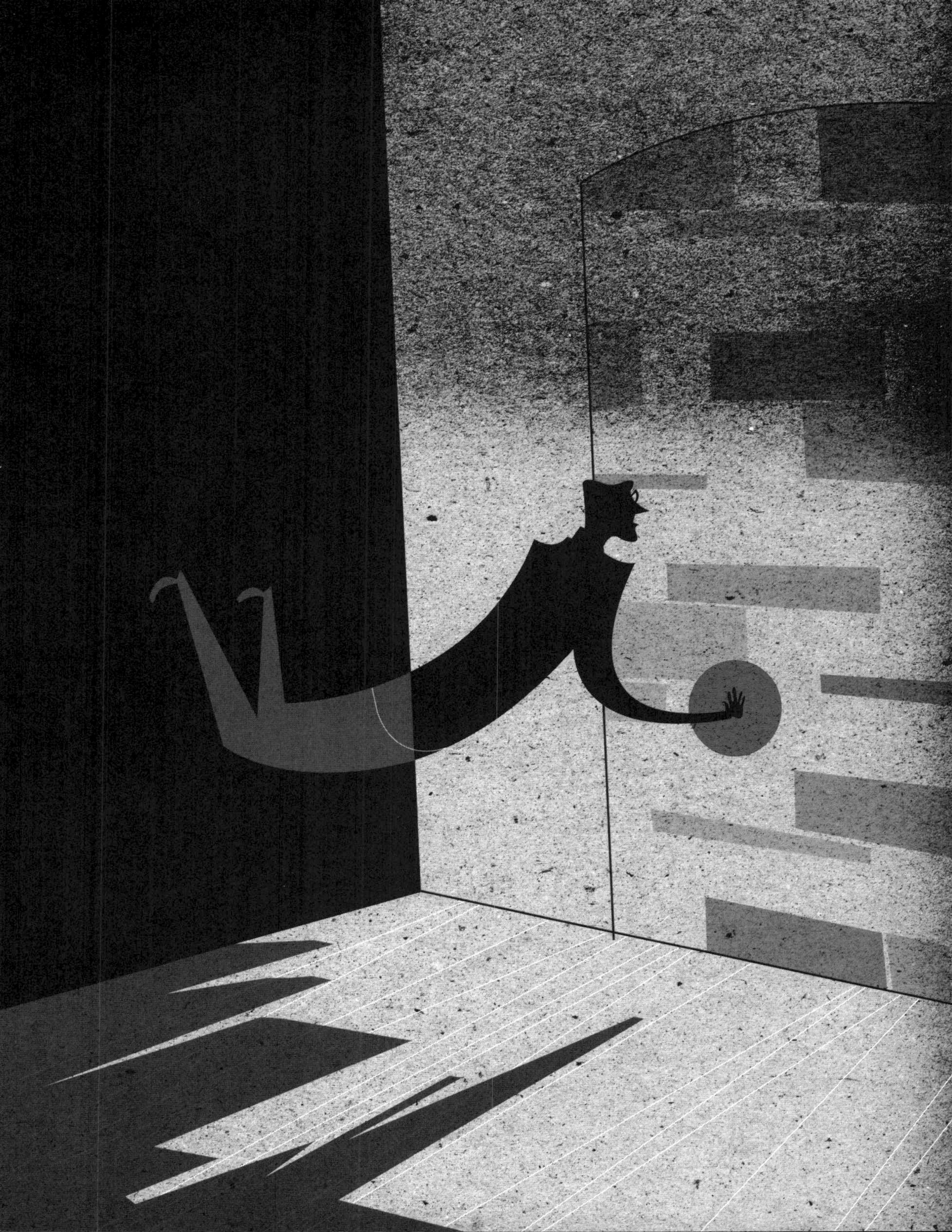

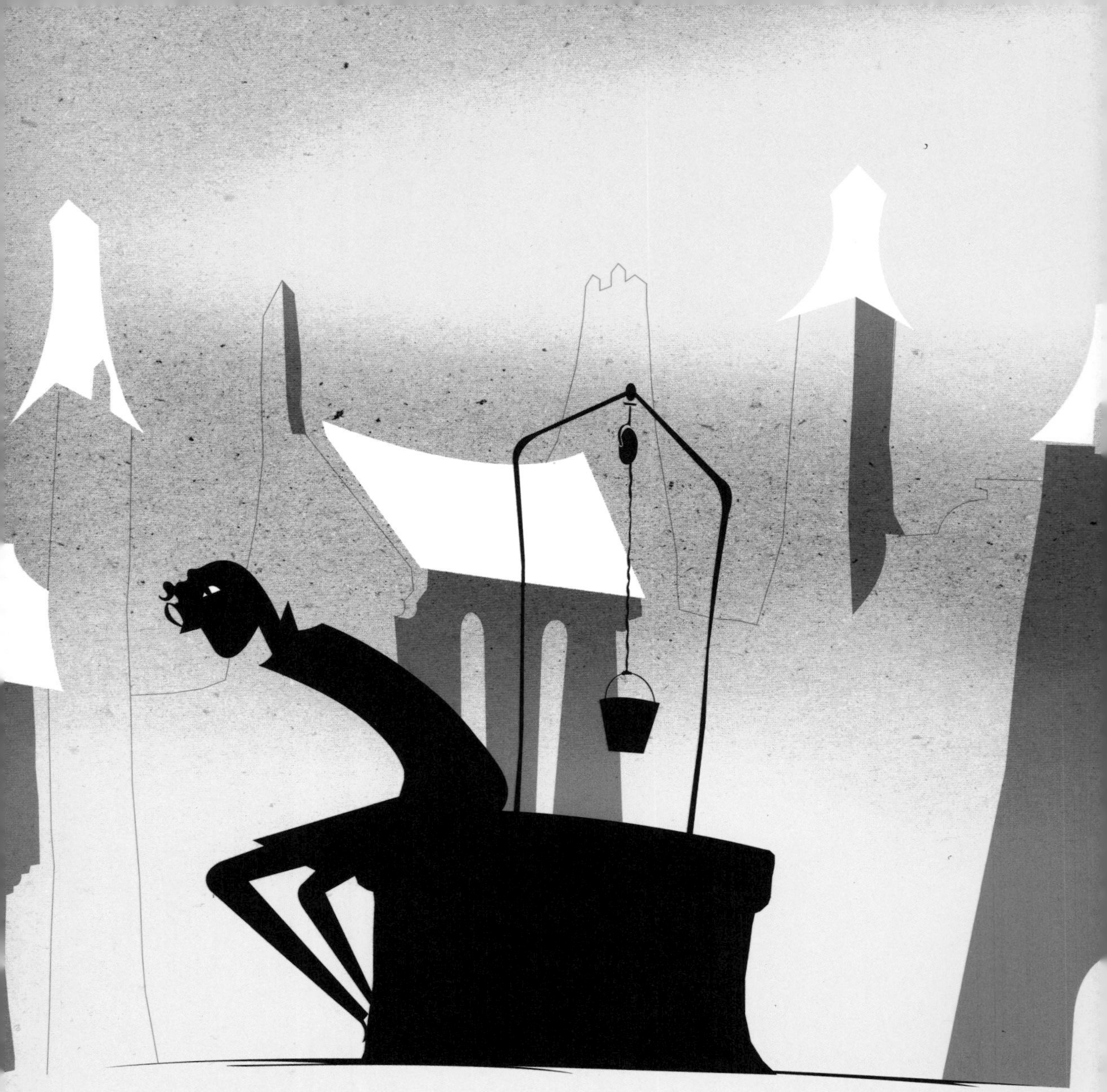

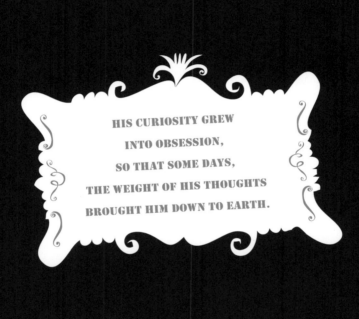

HIS CURIOSITY GREW
INTO OBSESSION,
SO THAT SOME DAYS,
THE WEIGHT OF HIS THOUGHTS
BROUGHT HIM DOWN TO EARTH.

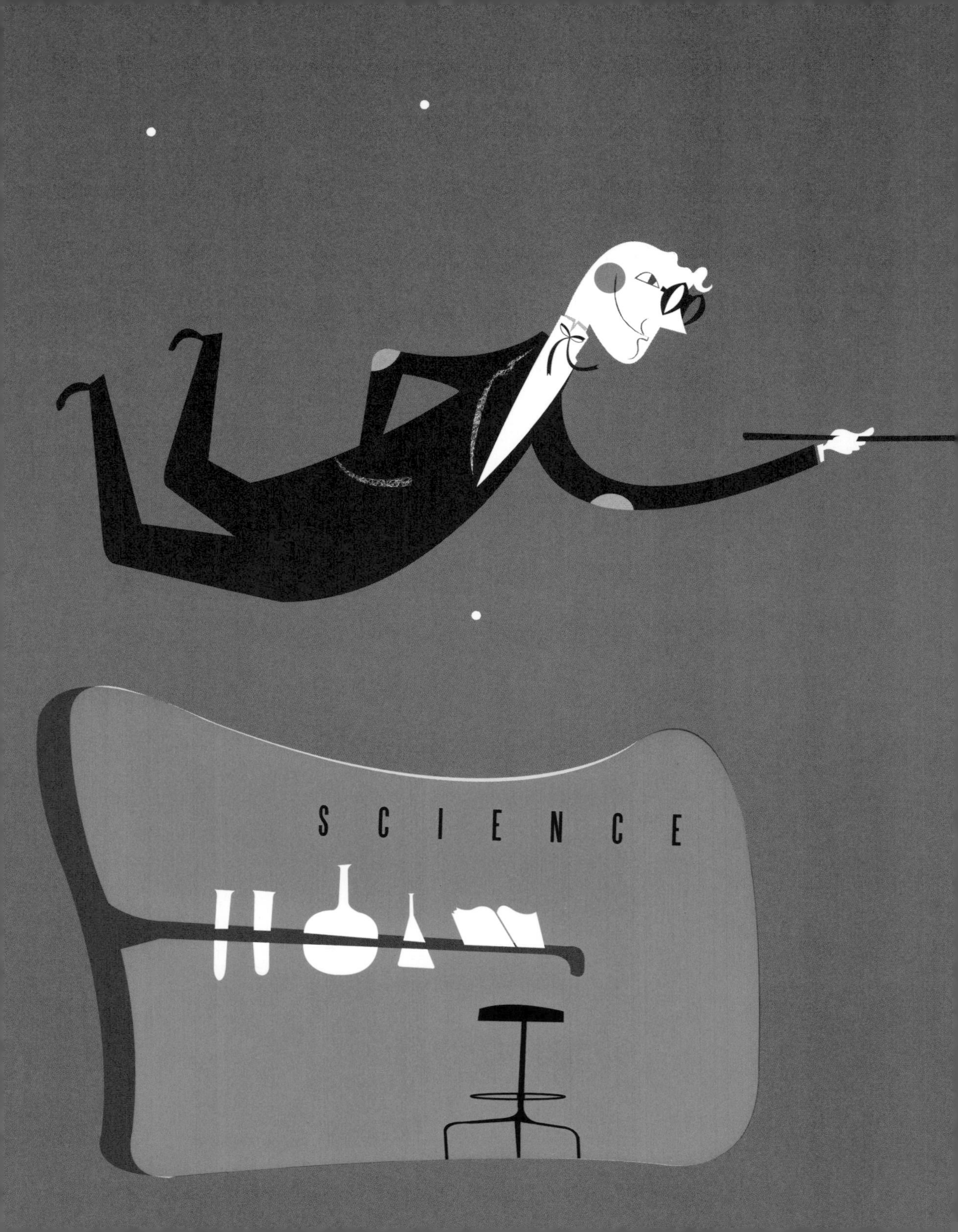
S C I E N C E

THE TOWN

MOUNTAIN

EARTH

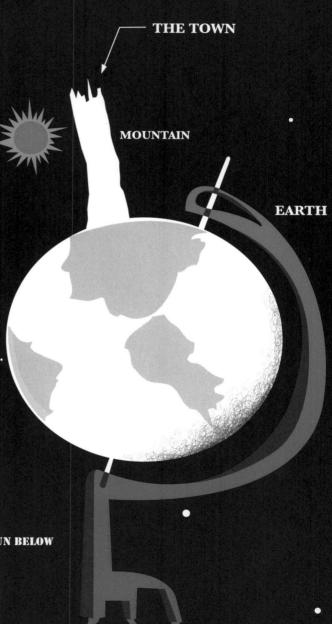

AFTER MONTHS
OF STUDY,
THE DISCOVERY!
ELATED,
THE TUTOR
REVEALED THE
KEY TO THE MYSTERY
TO BALONEY AND HIS DAUGHTER.
THE TOWN WAS LOCATED
AT SUCH GREAT ALTITUDE
THAT THE SUN,
EVEN AT ITS HIGHEST POINT,
WAS UNABLE TO SHINE
LIGHT AND WARMTH
UPON IT.
THE WALL HAD
CUT OFF THE TOWNSPEOPLE FROM THE SUN BELOW
WHICH WAS STILL THERE,
SIMPLY WAITING
TO BE LET IN.

BRANDISHING
PICKAXES AND HAMMERS,
THEY SET OUT TO MEET THE GREAT STAR
THAT SOME HAD ALMOST FORGOTTEN
AND OTHERS HAD NEVER SEEN.

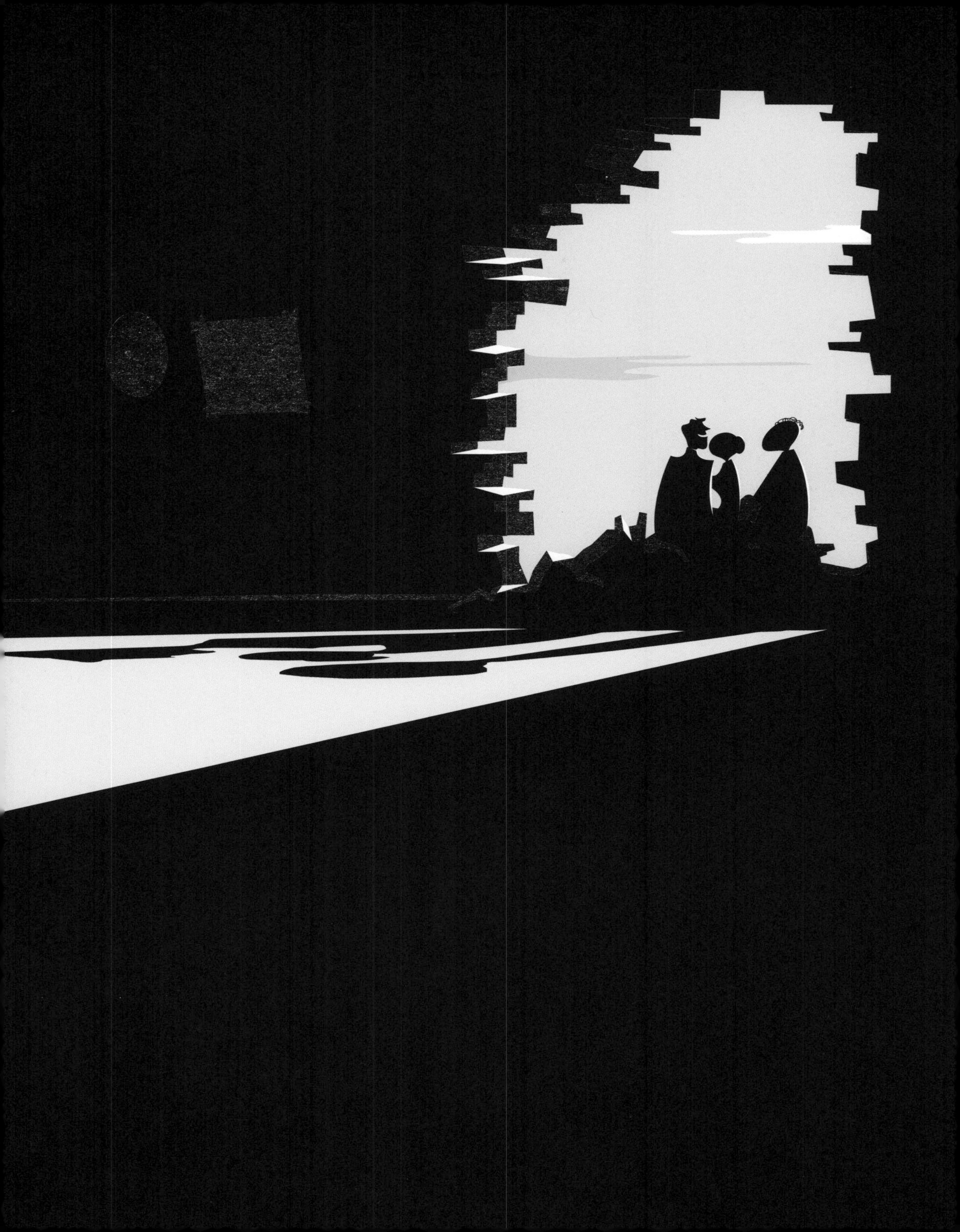

HORROR SEIZED THE DUKE
WHEN HE SAW A SLENDER RAY OF LIGHT
STRETCH OUT OVER HIS DESK.
FEARING THE WORST
FOR HIS LUCRATIVE HEATING ENTERPRISE,
HE CALLED FOR HIS CARRIAGE
TO BE MADE READY.

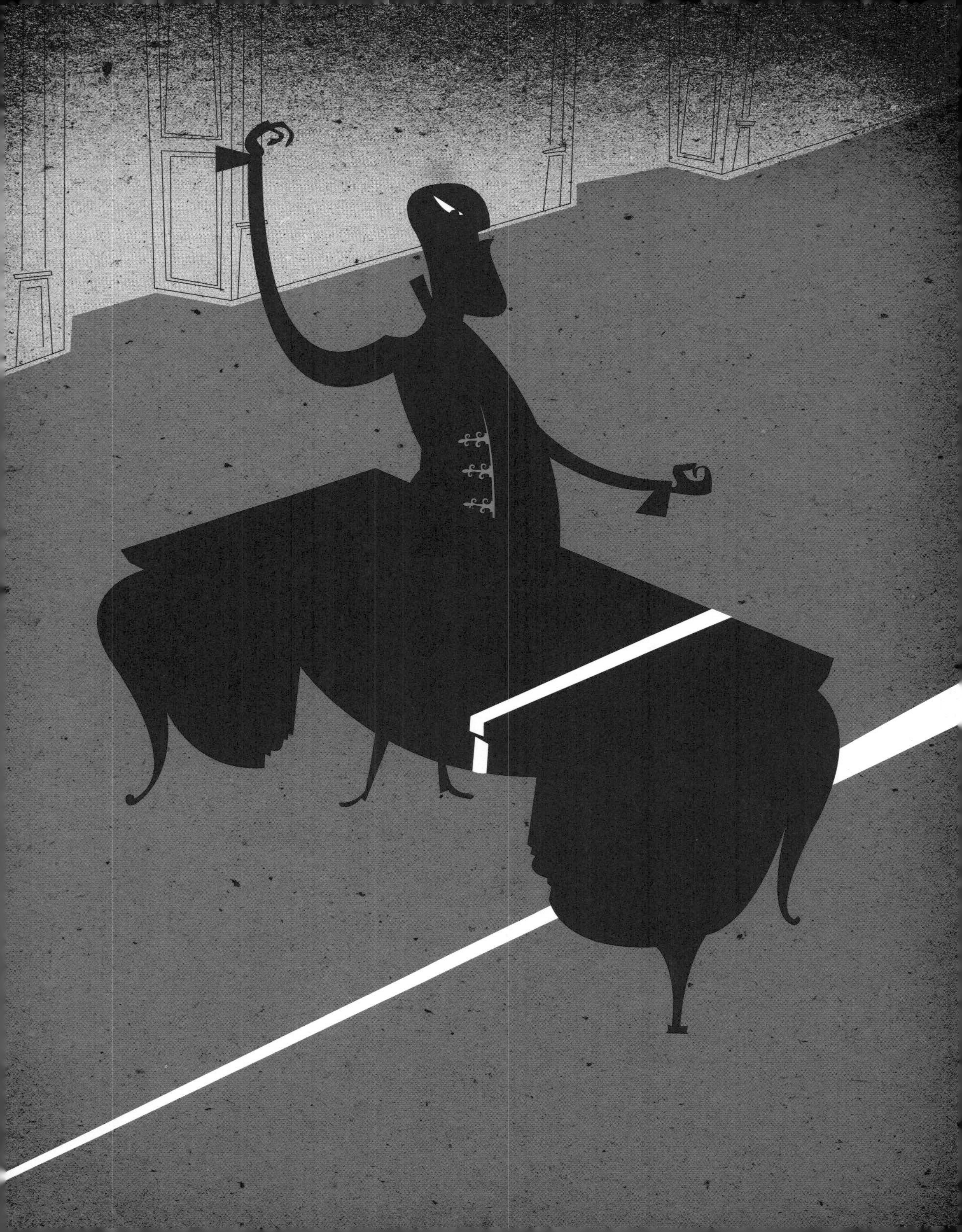

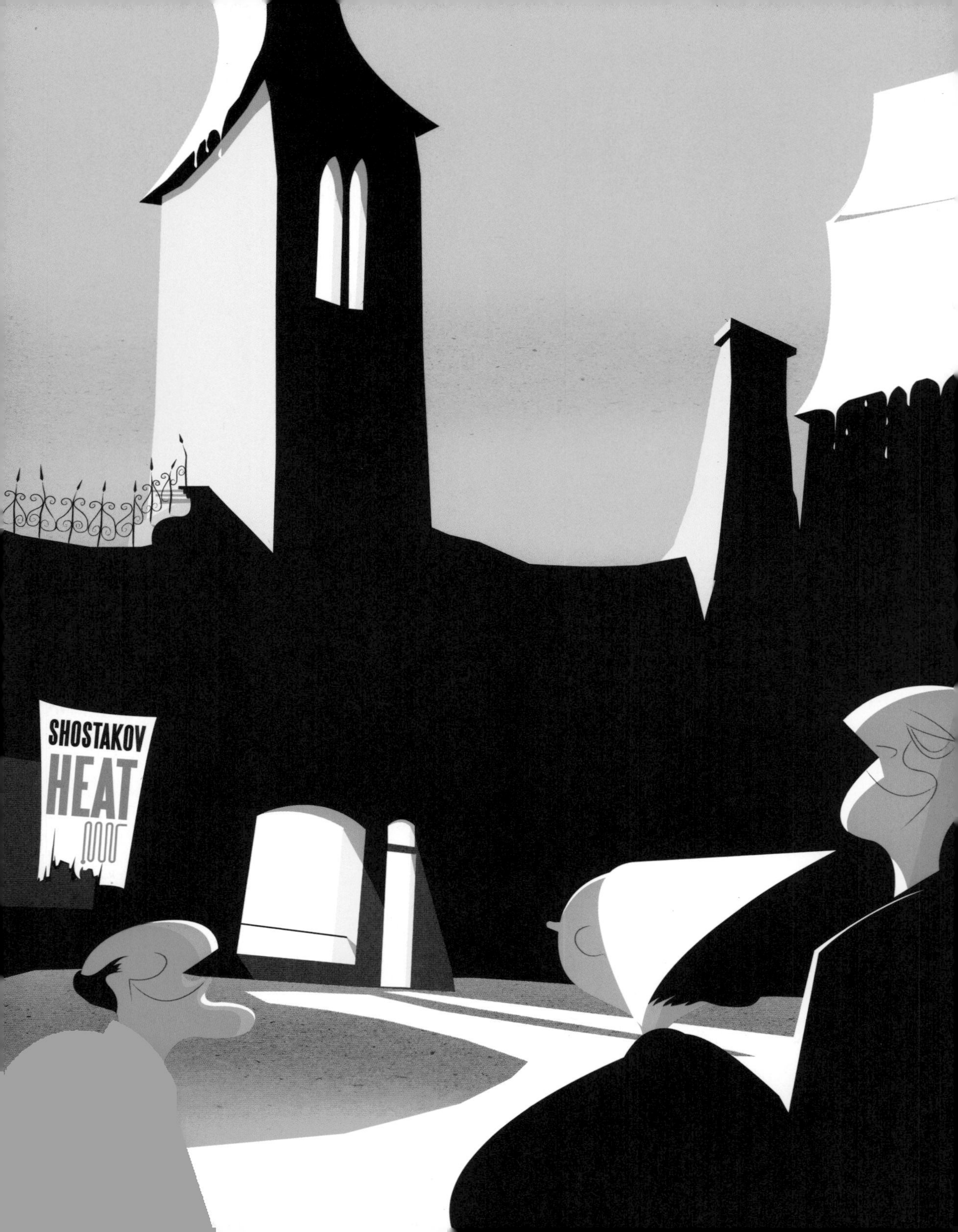
SHOSTAKOV
HEAT

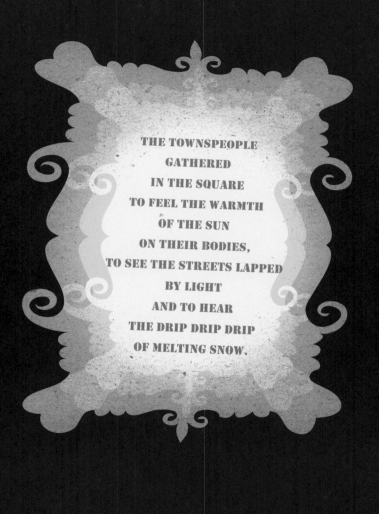

THE TOWNSPEOPLE
GATHERED
IN THE SQUARE
TO FEEL THE WARMTH
OF THE SUN
ON THEIR BODIES,
TO SEE THE STREETS LAPPED
BY LIGHT
AND TO HEAR
THE DRIP DRIP DRIP
OF MELTING SNOW.

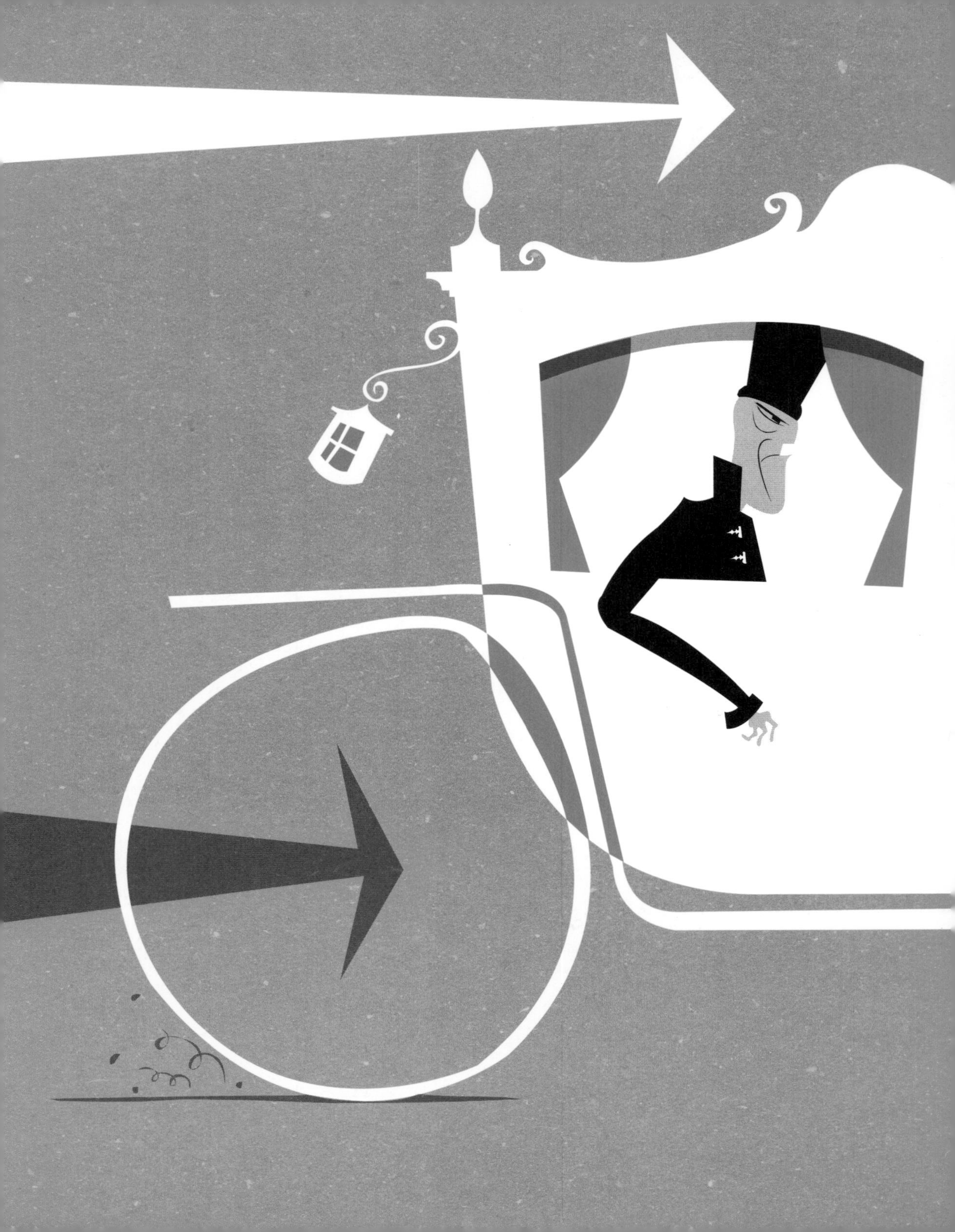

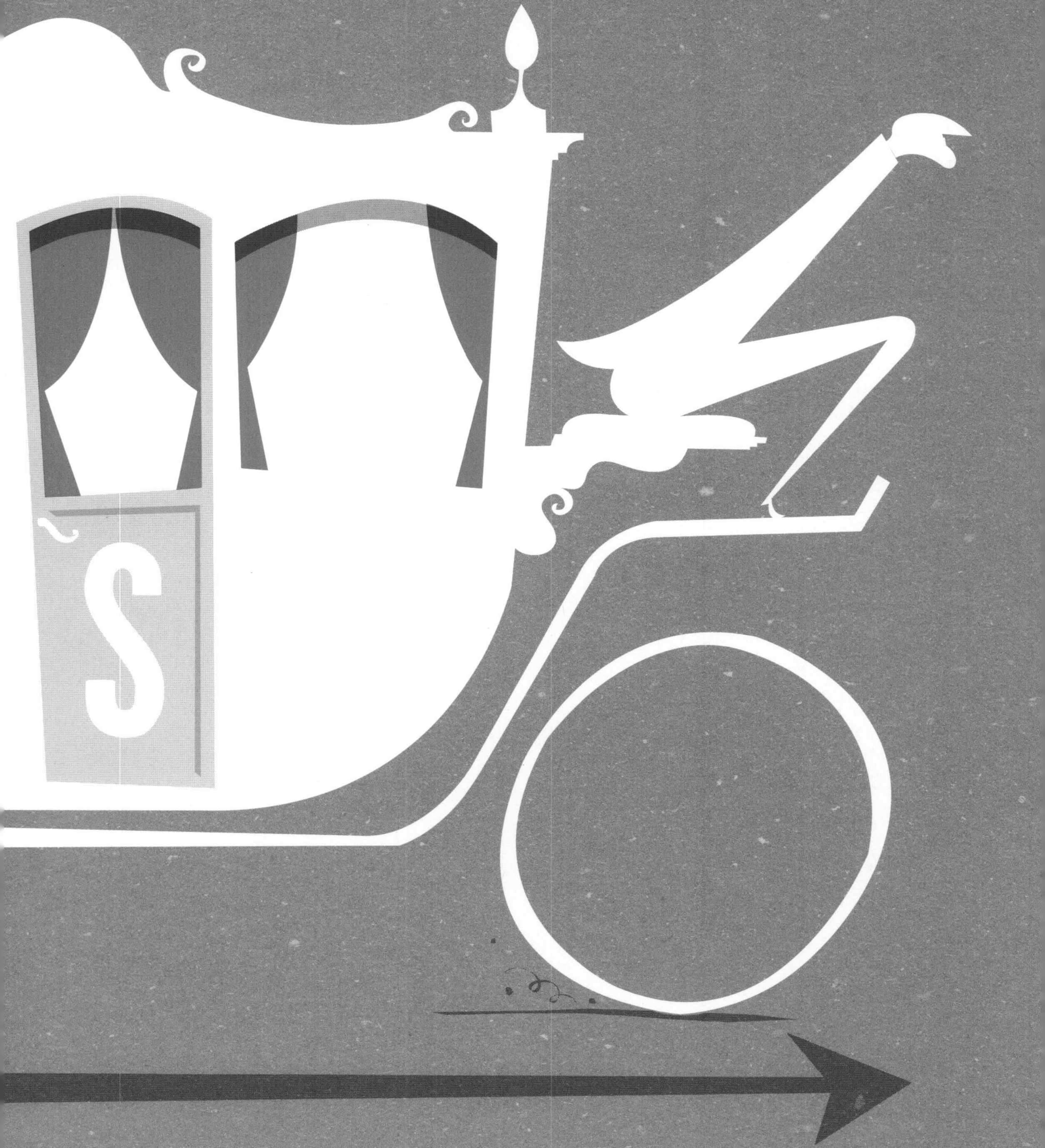
S

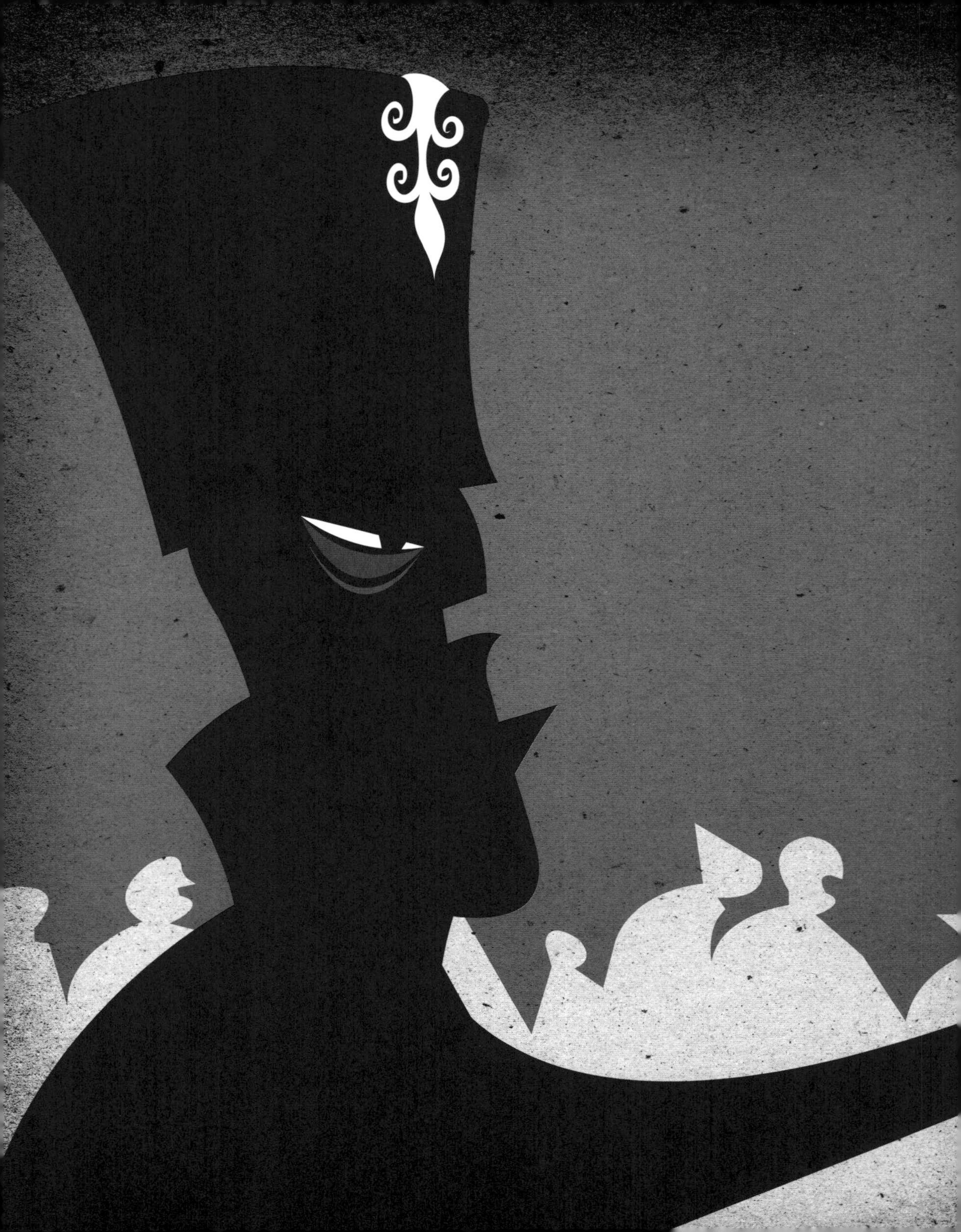

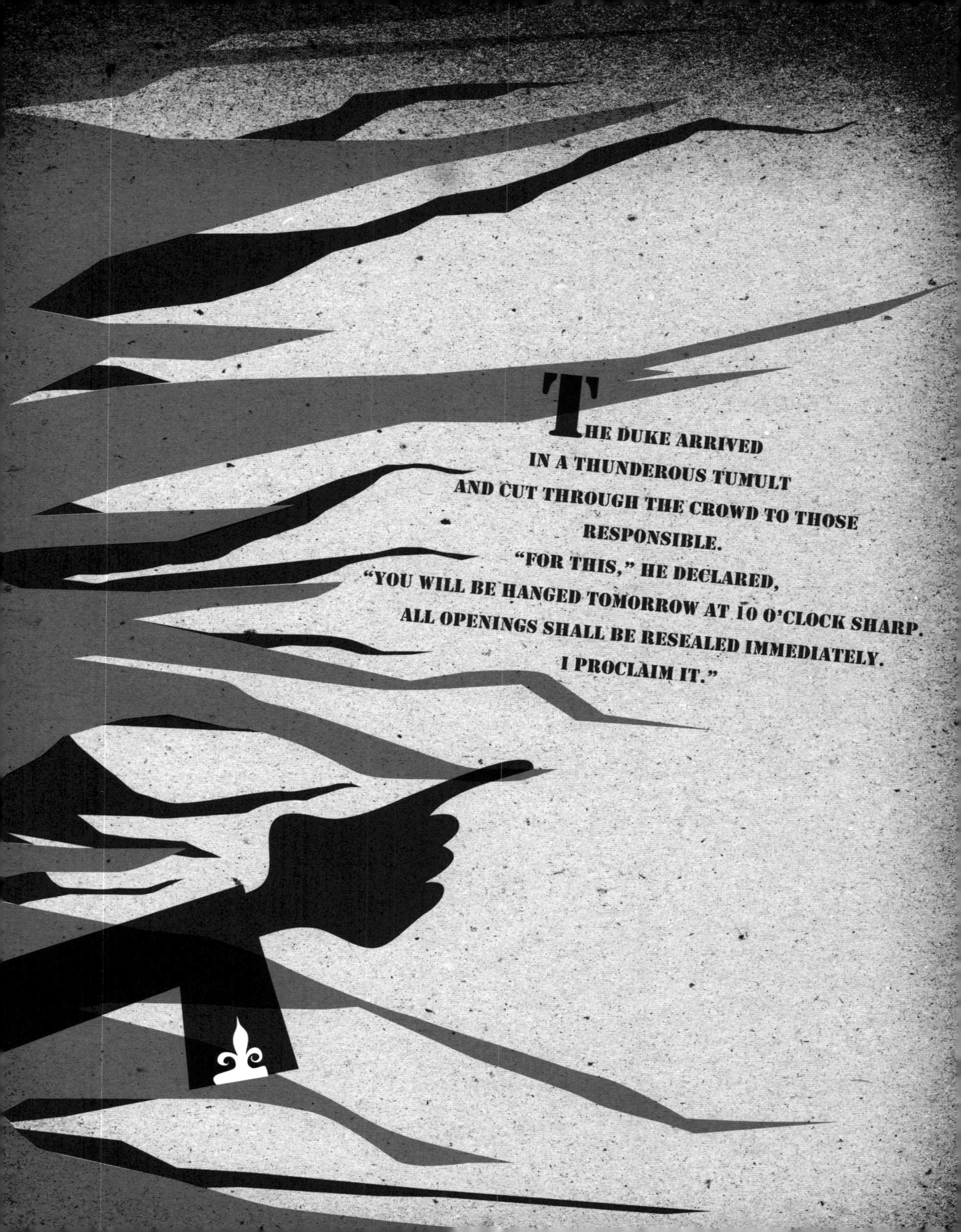

THE DUKE ARRIVED
IN A THUNDEROUS TUMULT
AND CUT THROUGH THE CROWD TO THOSE
RESPONSIBLE.
"FOR THIS," HE DECLARED,
"YOU WILL BE HANGED TOMORROW AT 10 O'CLOCK SHARP.
ALL OPENINGS SHALL BE RESEALED IMMEDIATELY.
I PROCLAIM IT."

Oh neighbors, grieve,
a black band tied around your arms,
for the lovers are dead.

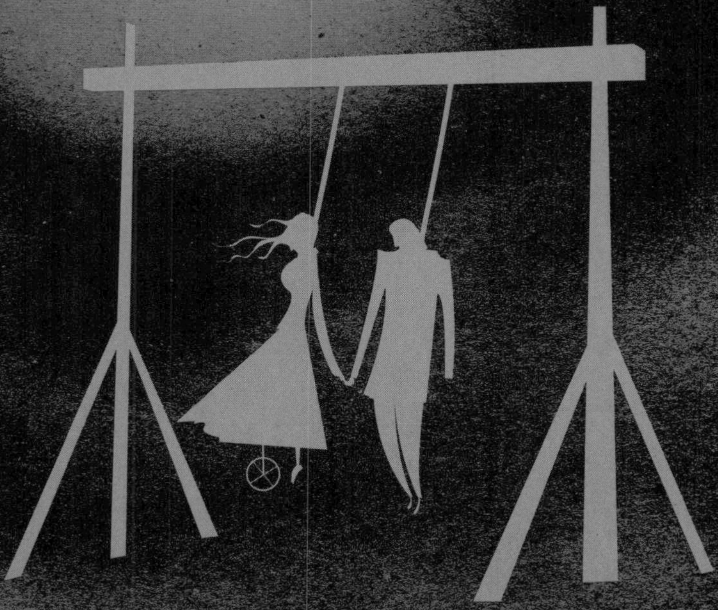

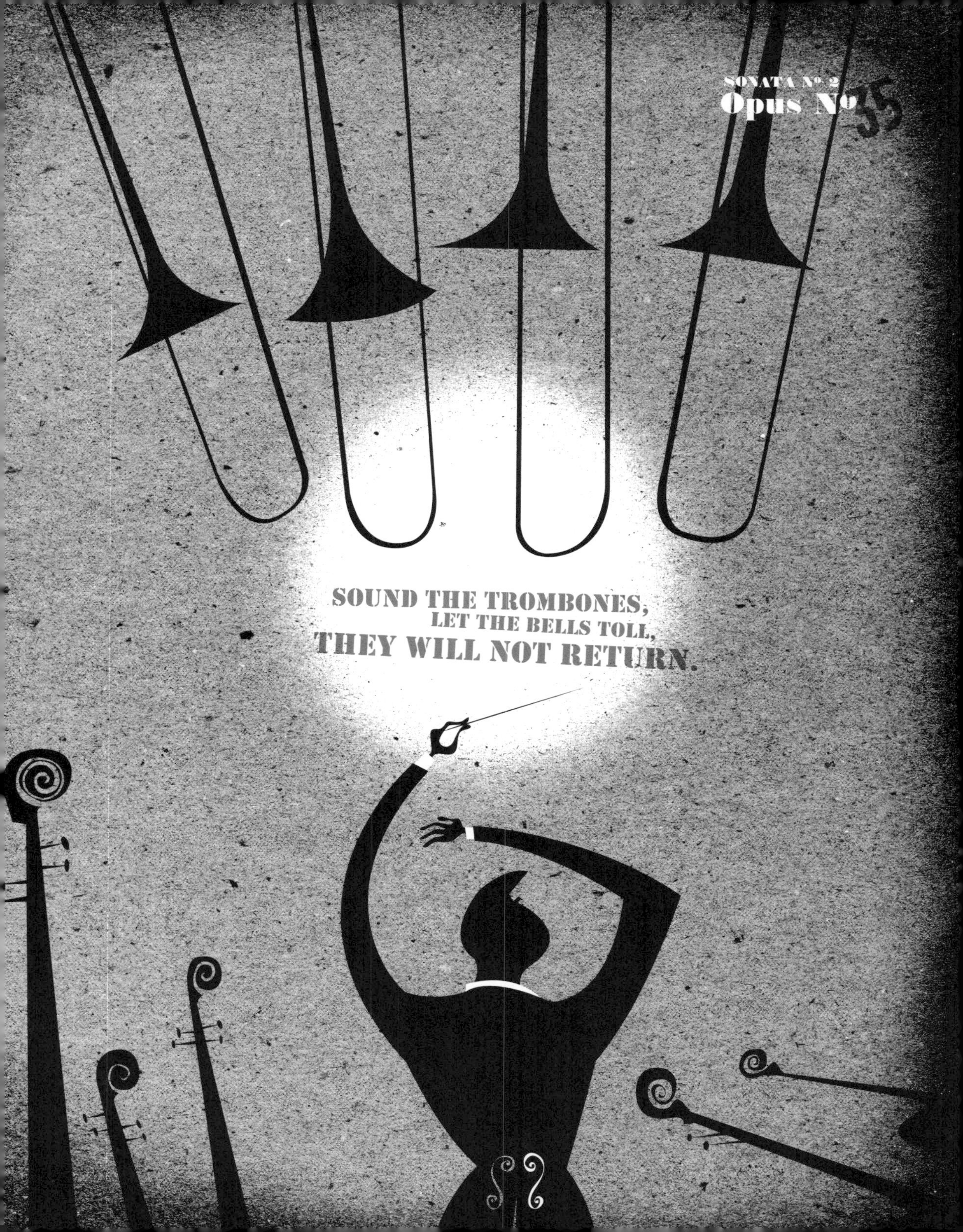
SONATA Nº 2
Opus Nº 35
SOUND THE TROMBONES,
LET THE BELLS TOLL,
THEY WILL NOT RETURN.

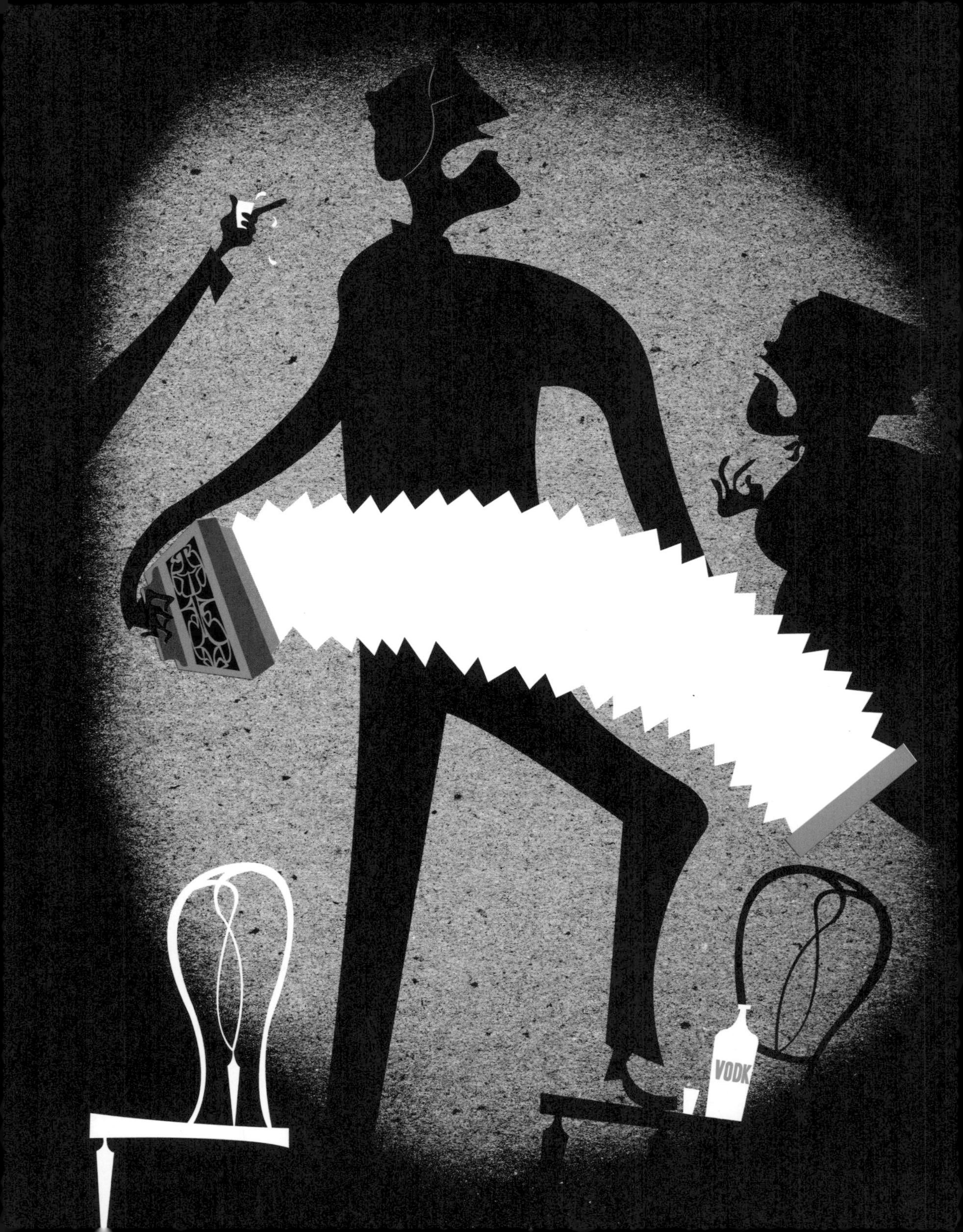
VODK

THAT EVENING,
SORROW WAS DRUNK BY ALL
AS THEY SANG WITH WRATH AND DANCED WITH GRIEF.
A FINAL FAREWELL
WAS OFFERED
TO THE DARK-EYED BEAUTY
AND HER BELOVED.

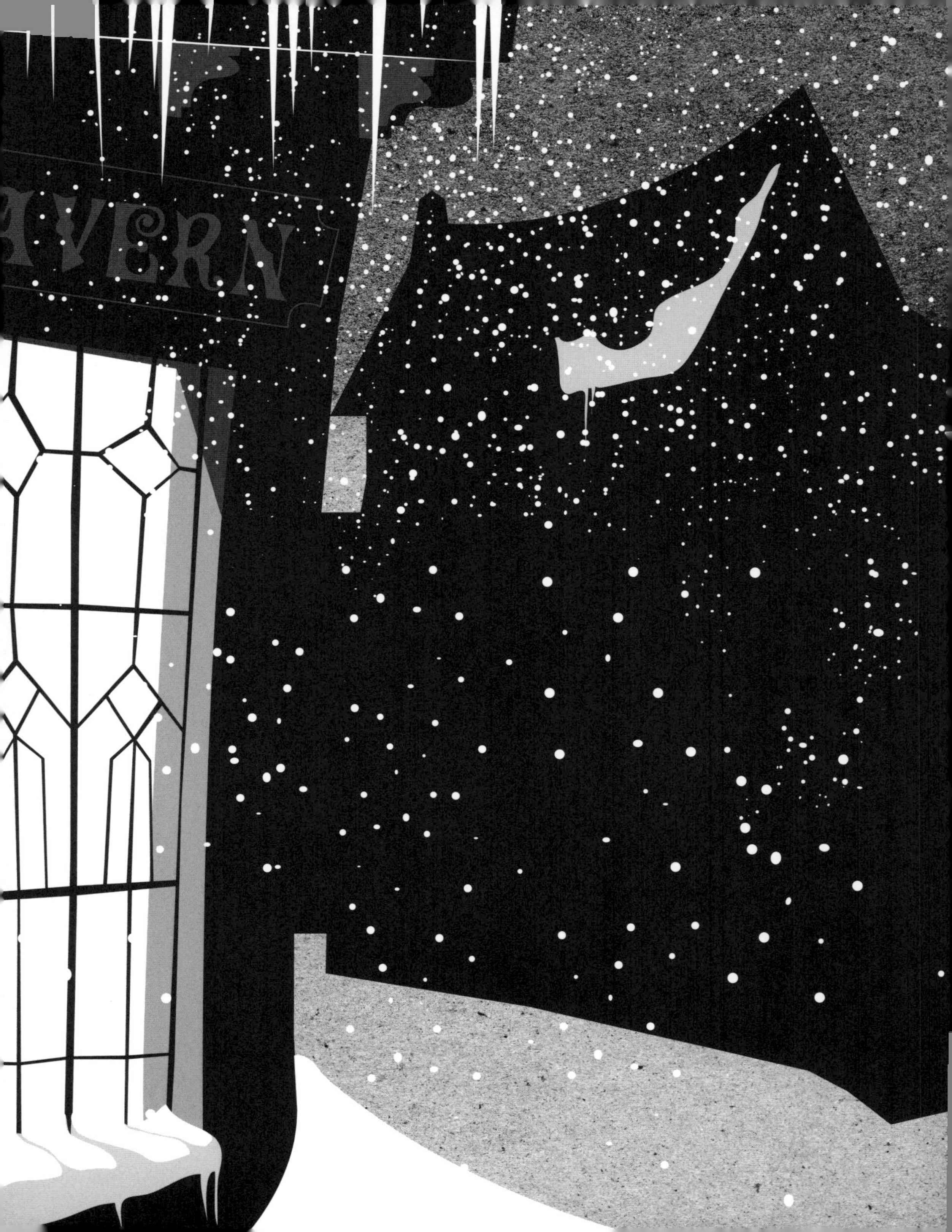
AVERN

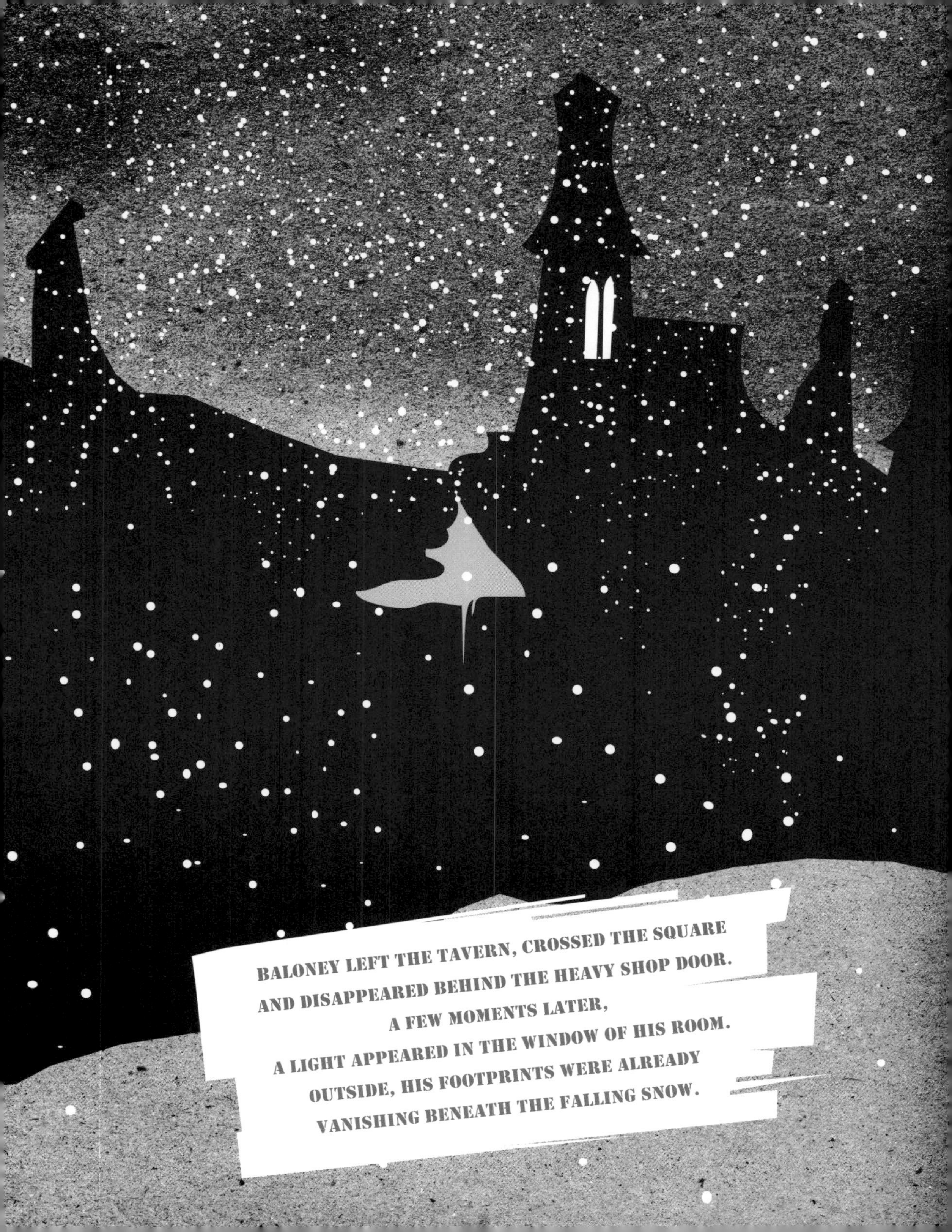
BALONEY LEFT THE TAVERN, CROSSED THE SQUARE
AND DISAPPEARED BEHIND THE HEAVY SHOP DOOR.
A FEW MOMENTS LATER,
A LIGHT APPEARED IN THE WINDOW OF HIS ROOM.
OUTSIDE, HIS FOOTPRINTS WERE ALREADY
VANISHING BENEATH THE FALLING SNOW.

AND IN THE COLD NIGHT
THE FINAL CALL CAME TO HIM
CARRIED BY THE WIND...

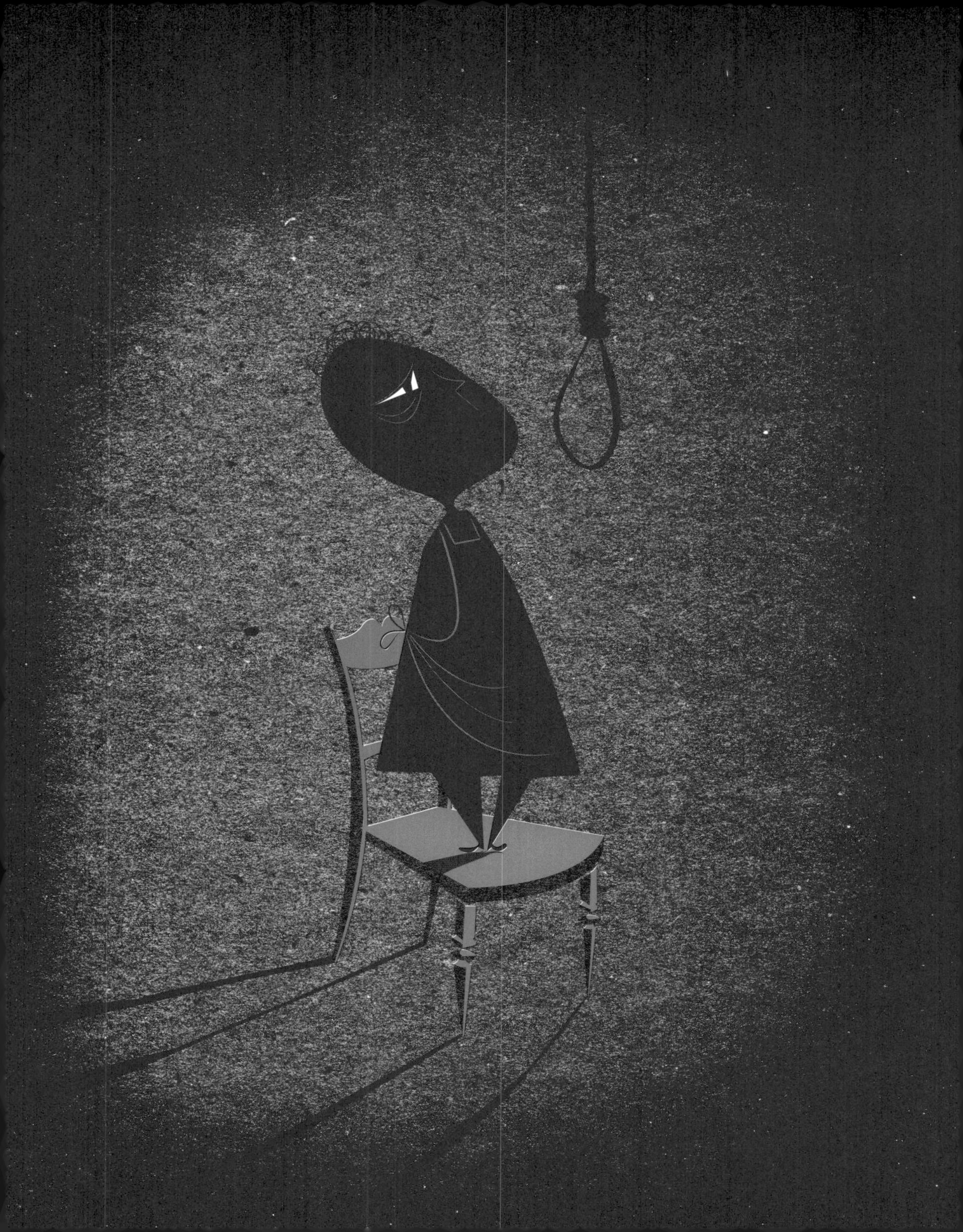

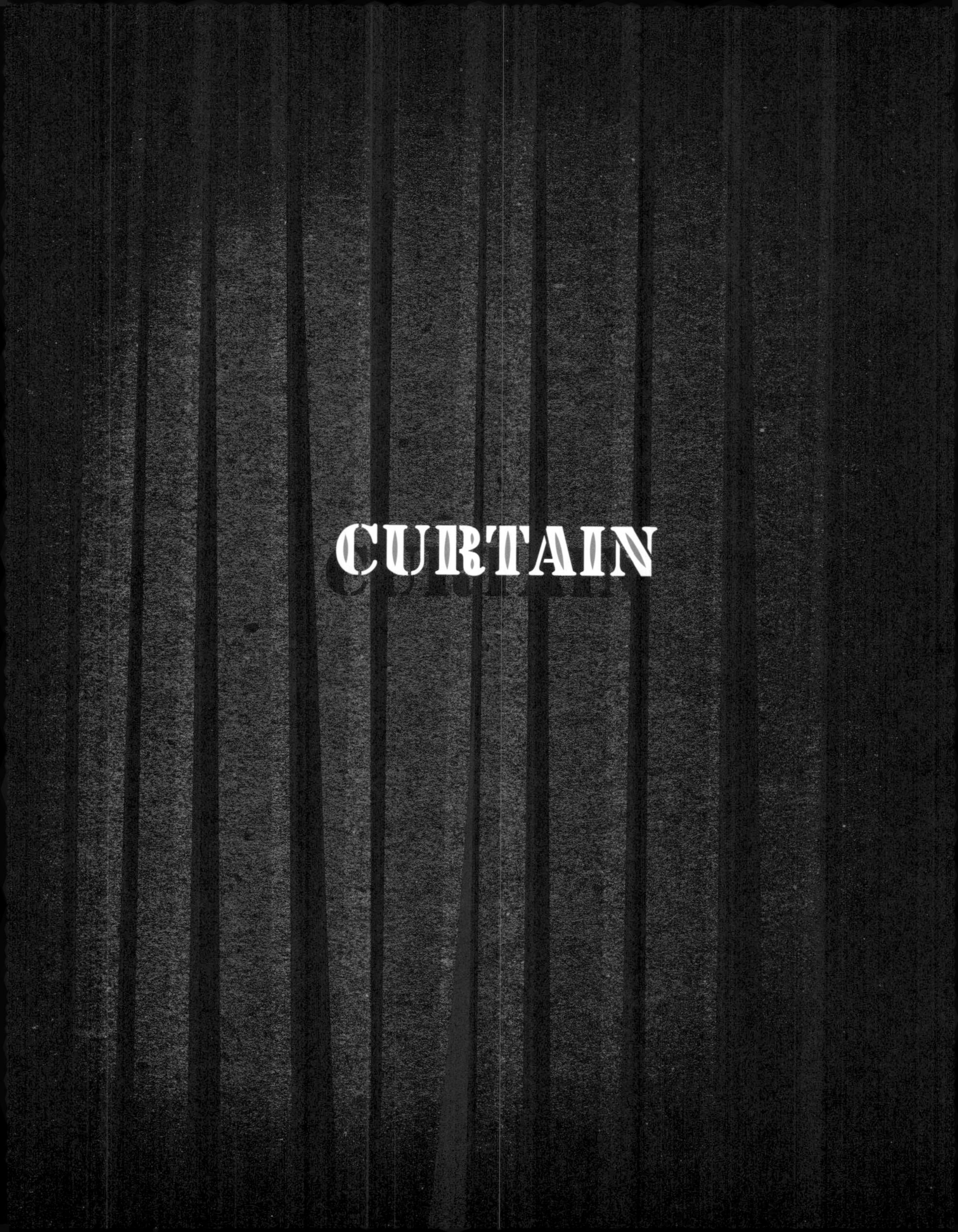
CURTAIN

PLAYLIST

- Overture...Shostakovich, Jazz Suite No. 2, VI, Waltz No. 2
- Baloney's lament.....................Anniversary Song, sung by: Al Jolson
- His daughter.........Prokofiev, Cinderella, Act II, Arrival at the Ball
- Baloney's nightmare.............Prokofiev, Cinderella, Act II, Midnight
- Birthday..................................Prokofiev, Lieutenant Kijé, Op. 60, II
- The Duke..Shostakovich, The Bolt, Suite From The Ballet, Op. 27a, III
- Time passes.................Shostakovich, Sophia Perouskaya, Op. 132
- The tutor's arrival..............Prokofiev, Cinderella, Act I, The Clock
- Why?.....................................Shostakovich, Jazz Suite No. 1, I, Waltz
- The discovery......................Prokofiev, Lieutenant Kijé, Op. 60, IV
- The star...............Kurt Weill, Symphony No. 2, Sostenuto-Allegro Molto
- The gallows...................Chopin, Sonata No. 2, Op. 35, III, Funeral March
- Finale........................Shostakovich, Jazz Suite No. 2, II, Lyric Waltz

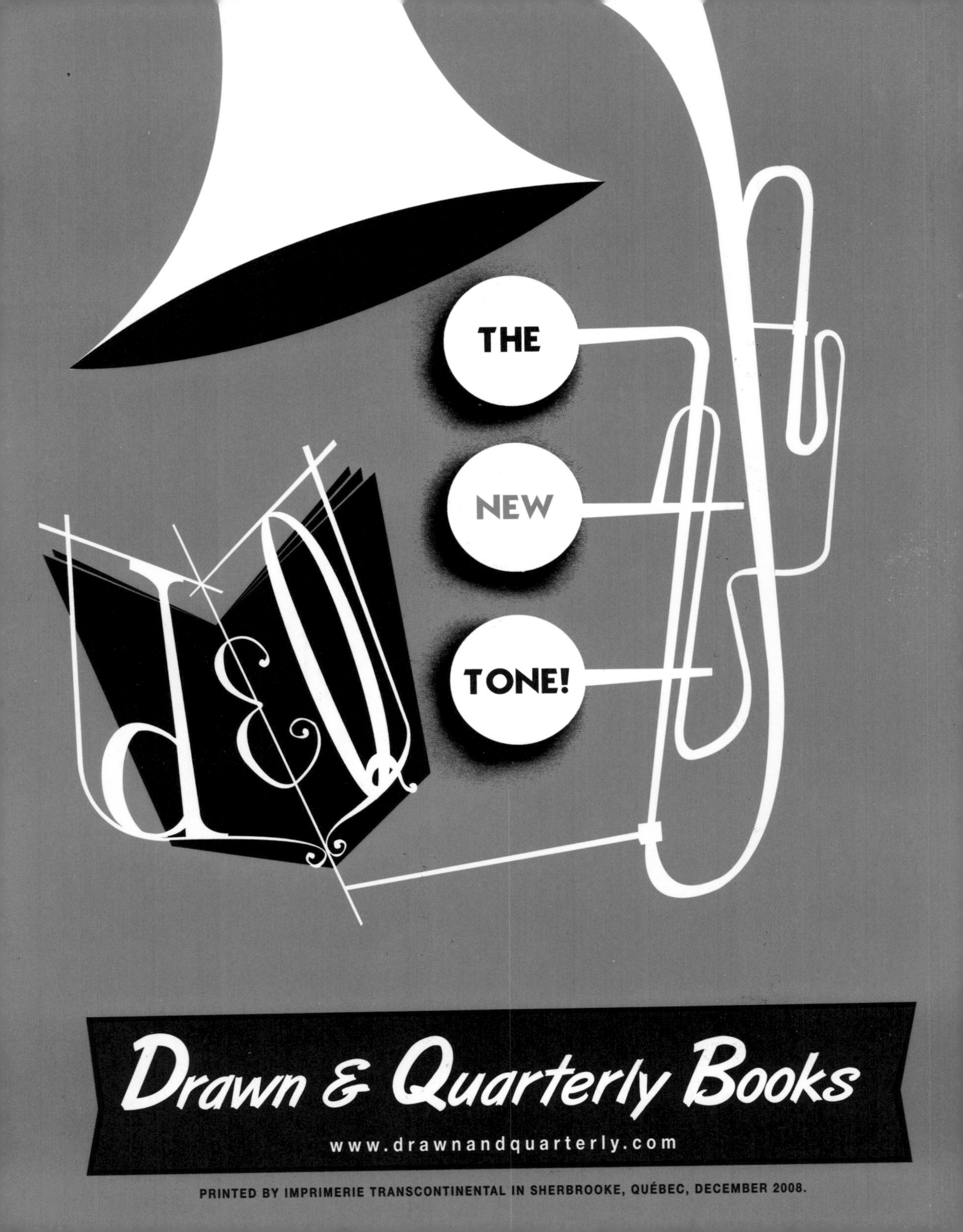
THE
NEW
TONE!

PRINTED BY IMPRIMERIE TRANSCONTINENTAL IN SHERBROOKE, QUÉBEC, DECEMBER 2008.